Mercury Bioaccumulation in Fishes from Subalpine Lakes in the Wallowa-Whitman National Forest, Northeastern Oregon and Western Idaho

By Collin A. Eagles-Smith, Garth Herring, Branden L. Johnson, U.S. Geological Survey; and Rick Graw, U.S. Forest Service

Open-File Report 2013–1148

U.S. Department of the Interior
U.S. Geological Survey

U.S. Department of the Interior
SALLY JEWELL, Secretary

U.S. Geological Survey
Suzette M. Kimball, Acting Director

U.S. Geological Survey, Reston, Virginia: 2013

For more information on the USGS—the Federal source for science about the Earth, its natural and living resources, natural hazards, and the environment—visit *http://www.usgs.gov* or call 1–888–ASK–USGS

For an overview of USGS information products, including maps, imagery, and publications, visit *http://www.usgs.gov/pubprod*

To order this and other USGS information products, visit *http://store.usgs.gov*

Suggested citation:
Eagles-Smith, C.A., Herring, G., Johnson, B.L., and Graw, R., 2013, Mercury bioaccumulation in fishes from subalpine lakes of the Wallowa-Whitman National Forest, northeastern Oregon and western Idaho: U.S. Geological Survey Open-File Report 2013-1148, 38 p.

Contents

Figures

Tables

Conversion Factors

Multiply	By	To obtain
Length		
centimeter (cm)	0.3937	inch (in.)
millimeter (mm)	0.03937	inch (in.)
meter (m)	3.281	foot (ft)
kilometer (km)	0.6214	mile (mi)
Area		
square meter (m^2)	10.76	square foot (ft^2)
hectare (ha)	0.003861	square mile (mi^2)
square kilometer (km^2)	0.3861	square mile (mi^2)
Volume		
liter (L)	0.264172	gallon (gal)
milliliter (mL)	0.0333814	ounce, fluid (fl. oz)
Mass		
gram (g)	0.03527	ounce, avoirdupois (oz)
milligram (mg)	0.00003527	ounce, avoirdupois (oz)
microgram (μg)	0.00000003527	ounce, avoirdupois (oz)

List of Acronyms

dw	dry weight
ww	wet weight
Hg	mercury
MeHg	methylmercury
SE	standard error
THg	total mercury

Temperature in degrees Celsius (°C) may be converted to degrees Fahrenheit (°F) as follows: °F=(1.8×°C)+32

Mercury Bioaccumulation in Fishes from Subalpine Lakes in the Wallowa-Whitman National Forest, Northeastern Oregon and Western Idaho

By Collin A. Eagles-Smith, Garth Herring, Branden L. Johnson, U.S. Geological Survey, and Rick Graw, U.S. Forest Service

Executive Summary

Mercury (Hg) is a globally distributed pollutant that poses considerable risks to human and wildlife health. Over the past 150 years since the advent of the industrial revolution, approximately 80 percent of global emissions have come from anthropogenic sources, largely fossil fuel combustion. As a result, atmospheric deposition of Hg has increased by up to 4-fold above pre-industrial times. Because of their isolation, remote high-elevation lakes represent unique environments for evaluating the bioaccumulation of atmospherically deposited Hg through freshwater food webs, as well as for evaluating the relative importance of Hg loading versus landscape influences on Hg bioaccumulation. The increase in Hg deposition to these systems over the past century, coupled with their limited exposure to direct anthropogenic disturbance make them useful indicators for estimating how changes in Hg emissions may propagate to changes in Hg bioaccumulation and ecological risk. In this study, we evaluated Hg concentrations in fishes of high-elevation, sub-alpine lakes in the Wallowa-Whitman National Forest in northeastern Oregon and western Idaho. Our goals were to (1) assess the magnitude of Hg contamination in small-catchment lakes to evaluate the risk of atmospheric Hg to human and wildlife health, (2) quantify the spatial variability in fish Hg concentrations, and (3) determine the ecological, limnological, and landscape factors that are best correlated with fish total mercury (THg) concentrations in these systems. Across the 28 study lakes, mean THg concentrations of resident salmonid fishes varied as much as 18-fold among lakes. Importantly, our top statistical model explained 87 percent of the variability in fish THg concentrations among lakes with four key landscape and limnological variables— catchment conifer density (basal area of conifers within a lake's catchment), lake surface area, aqueous dissolved sulfate, and dissolved organic carbon. The basal area of conifers within a lake's catchment was by far the most important variable explaining fish THg concentrations, with an increase in THg concentrations of more than 400 percent across the forest density spectrum. Across all study lakes, fish THg concentrations ranged from 0.004 to 0.438 milligrams per kilogram wet weight (mg/kg ww). Only a single individual fish sample exceeded the U.S. Environmental Protection Agency's (USEPA) human health tissue residue criteria of 0.3 mg/kg ww. However, 54 percent of fish (N=177) exceeded the more stringent tissue residue criteria (0.04 mg/kg ww) adopted by the Oregon Department of Environmental Quality to better protect subsistence fishers. Additionally, 2 and 10 percent of fish exceeded levels associated with reduced common loon reproduction and behavior, respectively. Whereas 25 and 68 percent of fish sampled exceeded concentrations deemed protective of mink and kingfisher, respectively. These results suggest that THg concentrations may be present in these lakes at levels associated with ecological risk. It is important to note however, that accurate inference on potential impairment cannot be made within the context of this study design and further research is needed to better quantify these risks.

Introduction and Objectives

Mercury (Hg) is a globally distributed pollutant that poses considerable risks to human and wildlife health (Scheuhammer and others, 2007). Under appropriate biogeochemical conditions in aquatic ecosystems, inorganic Hg is microbially converted to the highly toxic and bioavailable organic form, methylmercury (MeHg), which biomagnifies through food webs where it can reach toxicologically relevant concentrations in top predators. As a result, the ecological risk of Hg is driven by a combination of both inorganic loading, as well as ecological parameters that facilitate MeHg production and bioaccumulation. Inland lakes are particularly vulnerable to Hg contamination because they are recipients of transported Hg, and their organic rich, anoxic sediments can promote MeHg production.

Lakes receive Hg from various sources, including atmospheric deposition, watershed runoff, and glacial meltwater (St. Louis and others, 1994; Rudd, 1995). Over the past 150–200 years since the advent of the industrial revolution, approximately 80 percent of global emissions have come from anthropogenic sources, largely fossil fuel combustion (Mason and others, 1994), but also gold mining, and manufacturing (Pirrone and others, 2010). Mercury also is re-emitted to the atmosphere from forest fires and agricultural burning (Friedli and others, 2003). As a result, atmospheric deposition of Hg in remote environments has increased by approximately 3-fold (Lindberg and others, 2007). Importantly, there is substantial variability in the spatial patterns of anthropogenic Hg releases and deposition at local, regional, and global scales, associated with coal-fired power plants, industrial activity, and mining (Engstrom and others, 2007), as well as in the propensity of inorganic Hg to be methylated across the landscape. Therefore, it can be difficult to determine how much of the variability in Hg concentrations among systems can be attributed to Hg loading relative to in situ MeHg production.

Because of their isolation, remote high elevation lakes represent unique environments for evaluating the bioaccumulation of atmospherically deposited Hg through freshwater food webs, as well as for evaluating the relative importance of Hg loading versus landscape influences on Hg bioaccumulation. The increase in Hg deposition to these systems over the past century (Phillips and others, 2011), coupled with their limited exposure to direct anthropogenic disturbance make them useful indicators for estimating how changes in Hg emissions may propagate changes in Hg bioaccumulation and ecological risk. In this study, we evaluated Hg bioaccumulation in fishes of high elevation, sub-alpine lakes in the Wallowa-Whitman National Forest in northeastern Oregon and western Idaho (fig. 1). Our goals were to (1) assess the magnitude of Hg contamination in a collection of small catchment lakes to evaluate the risk of atmospherically deposited Hg to human and wildlife health, (2) quantify the spatial variability in fish Hg concentration across these lakes, and (3) determine the ecological, limnological, and landscape factors that are most strongly related to fish THg concentrations.

Methods

Site Description and Field Collection

The Wallowa-Whitman National Forest (WWNF) occupies more than 9,000 km^2 of land, including nearly 2,500 km^2 of designated wilderness. The forest is comprised of varied landscapes including low-elevation grasslands, coniferous forests, and alpine meadows. High-elevation habitats are found in the Elkhorn Mountains, the Wallowa Mountains and Eagle Cap Wilderness, and the Hells Canyon National Recreation Area. A common feature in the mountains across the WWNF is small (<0.5 km^2), high-elevation (>2,000 m) lakes within isolated catchments that are (or were historically) stocked for recreational purposes with non-native salmonid fishes, such as brook trout (*Salvelinus fontinalis*) or rainbow trout (*Oncorhynchus mykiss*) (fig. 2). These lakes are solely catchment or groundwater fed, and Hg sources are likely limited primarily to atmospheric deposition because they do not have inflowing streams. The catchments associated with these lakes generally are small (< 5 km), and are comprised of a combination of open, rocky terrain, and temperate, subalpine coniferous forest.

Using the U.S. Forest Service limnology database, we selected 28 individual lakes within 5 different regions of the WWNF (table 1, fig. 3). To select lakes for sampling, we identified those with records of self-sustaining populations of brook trout, rainbow trout, or cutthroat trout (*Oncorhynchus clarkii*), and that also occurred within a 1-day hike from a trailhead. We then divided these lakes into geographic regions: North Elkhorn, South Elkhorn, North Eagle Cap, South Eagle Cap, and Seven Devils (fig. 3) based on their geography, and randomly selected 7 lakes per region to sample. We targeted 7 lakes per region because our goal was a total of 25 lakes and we assumed that fish may no longer be present in some lakes with historical reports of fish presence.

Between July 11 and September 1, 2011, fishes were collected in association with ongoing, regular U.S. Forest Service and Oregon Department of Fish and Wildlife fish monitoring programs from 28 lakes in the Wallowa-Whitman National Forest. At each lake, rainbow trout, brook trout, cutthroat trout, or lake trout (*Salvelinus namaycush*) were sampled using hook and line and 30 × 2 m variable-mesh gillnets. We wrapped collected fish in clean, solvent-rinsed aluminum foil and then sealed them in individually labeled polyethylene bags. Each fish was kept cool on ice or snow until delivery to the laboratory, where they were stored at -20°C. At 21 of the lakes, we also collected water samples in 125 mL acid-cleaned amber glass bottles. To minimize sediment disturbance and contamination of the sample with particulate material, we sampled from the shoreline of lakes (at the outflow if applicable), making sure we were standing on an emerging solid object, such as a rock or log. We uncapped each clean bottle underwater, and rinsed the bottle 3 times with lake water. On our final fill, we capped the bottle underwater and stored it on ice prior to shipment to the laboratory for filtration and chemical analysis.

Fish Sample Processing and Tissue Preparation

In the laboratory, we thawed each fish sample to room temperature, and then measured standard length to the nearest millimeter on a fish board and mass to the nearest 0.1 g on a digital balance. We calculated the body condition of each fish using the Relative Condition Factor (K_n), which accounts for potential changes in shape as fish grow (Anderson and Neumann, 1996). The relative condition factor was calculated as:

$$K_n = W/W',$$

Where: W = fish whole body mass, in g and,

W' = the predicted length-specific mean mass from a predictive length-mass regression model calculated for each species.

To determine W' for each species, we used $\log_{10}$-transformed standard length (mm) and log10-transformed wet mass (g) data for all fish of each species, from all lakes in which they were captured (brook trout linear regression: n = 230, r^2 = 0.96, intercept = -11.646, slope = 3.099; rainbow trout linear regression: n = 85, r^2 = 0.91, intercept = -10.696, slope = 2.913; cutthroat trout linear regression: n = 11, r^2 = 0.97, intercept = -10.520, slope = 2.854). We then removed sagittal otoliths from each fish, cleaned them with deionized water, and stored them in clean, dry vials until further processing. From each fish, we dissected 5–10 g of skinless axial muscle, rinsed the muscle tissue in deionized water, blotted it dry with a clean, lint-free wipe, and weighed it on an analytical balance to the nearest 0.0001 g. We then dried each muscle sample in a convection oven at 50°C for 48 h, or until a constant mass was achieved. We subsequently removed the samples from the drying oven and allowed them to cool to room temperature in a desiccator. Once cool, we measured the dry mass of each muscle tissue sample to the nearest 0.0001 g, and ground them to a fine powder in a tissue mill. The homogenized samples were then stored in a dark desiccator until chemical analyses.

Mercury Determination

We determined total mercury (THg) concentrations on the axial muscle of each fish sample because most (90–95 percent) of mercury in fish muscle tissue is in the methylmercury (MeHg) form (Bloom and others, 1992). Total Hg concentrations were determined following EPA method 7473 (U.S. Environmental Protection Agency, 2000) on a Milestone tri-cell DMA-80 Direct Mercury Analyzer (Milestone Inc, Monroe, Connecticut, USA) at the USGS Forest and Rangeland Science Center's Contaminant Ecology Laboratory in Corvallis, Oregon. Briefly, we used an integrated sequence of drying (250°C for 30s), thermal decomposition (650°C for 90s), catalytic conversion, and then amalgamation, followed by cold vapor atomic absorption spectroscopy. Unless stated otherwise, we analyzed and report all muscle tissue samples on a dry weight basis in order to control for variable moisture content among individuals, and because it is a more toxicologically relevant measure of THg concentrations. However, to facilitate comparison to other studies and to allow conversion to wet weight concentrations we determined moisture content in each sample. Moisture content in the fish muscle tissue ranged from 74.7 to 85.8 percent with a mean (± standard error) of 79.8 ± 0.1%.

Quality-assurance measures included analysis of two certified reference materials (either dogfish muscle tissue [DORM-3; National Research Council of Canada, Ottawa, Canada], or dogfish liver [DOLT-3; National Research Council of Canada, Ottawa, Canada], two system and method blanks, and two duplicates per batch of 30 samples. Recoveries (± standard error [SE]) averaged 99.4 ± 1.8 percent (n = 60) and 97.9 ± 0.8 percent (n = 90) for certified reference materials and calibration checks, respectively. Absolute relative percent difference for all duplicates averaged 3.4 ± 0.5 percent.

Stable Isotope Analysis

Analysis of carbon and nitrogen stable isotope ratios ($\delta^{13}C$ and $\delta^{15}N$, respectively), provide for a time integrated assessment of an organism's foraging ecology (Hobson and Bairlein, 2003). Specifically, carbon and nitrogen stable isotope ratios can provide a quantitative estimate of a fish's relative reliance on different carbon sources (for example, benthic vs. pelagic), as well as trophic position (Eagles-Smith and others, 2008). We analyzed stable isotope ratios of both elements in muscle tissue of each fish sampled. However, isotope ratios at the base of lake food webs often vary among lakes, making inter-lake comparisons of foraging ecology difficult using raw data (Post, 2002). Thus, isotope ratios in consumers need to be baseline adjusted for their specific lake though the analysis of isotope ratios in obligate primary consumers (Post, 2002). In this study, we were unable to collect adequate primary consumers across lakes, thus we constrain our interpretation of isotope data only to within-lake comparisons of individual fishes.

Stable-isotope analysis was performed on a continuous flow isotope ratio mass spectrometer (IRMS; dualinlet Europa 20/20, PDZ Europa, Crewe, UK) at the University of California, Davis Stable Isotope Facility. Approximately 0.80–1.20 mg of tissue were weighed and sealed into tin capsules. Sample combustion to CO^2 and N^2 occurred at 1,000°C in an inline elemental analyzer. A Carbosieve G column separated the gas before introduction into the IRMS. Standards (PeeDee Belemnite for $\delta^{13}C$ and air for $\delta^{15}N$) were injected directly into the IRMS before and after sample peaks. Isotope ratios are expressed in per mil (‰) notation. Using $\delta^{13}C$ as an example, ratios are defined by the following equation:

$$\delta^{13}C = \{[(^{13}C/^{12}C)\text{sample}/(^{13}C/^{12}C)\text{standard}] - 1\} \times 1{,}000.$$

Otolith Preparation and Fish Age Determination

We prepared otoliths for age determination through polishing in order to remove coarse material that can interfere with identifying annuli. We first mounted each otolith, with the sulcus facing up, to clear glass microscope slides using Loctite® cyanoacrylate adhesive. We polished each otolith with a series of sanding and polishing discs in order to remove overburden and expose the growth increments. We started with the coarse removal of external calcification and excess glue using 600 or 400 μm grit wet/dry sandpaper. Once the delicate internal structure of the otolith was revealed, we applied a sequential gradient of polishing paper (30, 15, 9, 2, 1 μm grit) to prepare the surface for visual assessment. Throughout the polishing step, we inspected the polished face of each otolith under a compound microscope (2.5× and 10× magnification) to ensure that sufficient polishing was occurring, and that otoliths were not overpolished, which results in reduction of growth increment visibility. Polishing was considered complete when growth increments were clearly visible from the margins to the nucleus. After polishing, we captured digital images of each otolith (fig. 4) at 10× magnification using a compound microscope equipped with a Leica® digital inline camera, connected to a desktop computer. We subsequently adjusted image quality as necessary using ImageJ software (Rasband, 1997) to facilitate identification of annual increments. We estimated the age of each fish by counting the sequence of transparent and opaque annuli along a plane from the nucleus to the margin, following Secor and others (1991). Two independent, blind readings were made, each by different people, and the age estimates were compared. Any otoliths with age estimates that were not in agreement were then interpreted by a third person. If the third reading was in agreement with either of the other two, then that age was accepted. If all three readings were different, then we used the mean age for the three readings.

Water Chemistry

All water samples were shipped immediately to the USDA Forest Service Air Program Biogeochemistry Laboratory in Fort Collins, Colorado. Prior to analysis water samples were filtered through 0.7-μm glass fiber filters under gentle vacuum. Conductivity and pH were determined with a Metrohm/Brinkman Model 712 conductivity meter and Metrohm/Brinkman Model 809 pH meter, respectively. Acid neutralizing capacity (ANC) was determined using the Gran analysis technique (Gran, 1952). Anions (F^-, Cl^-, NO_2^-, NO_3^-, SO_4^{2-}) and cations (Na^+, NH_4^+, K^+, Mg_2^+, Ca_2^+) were measured with a Metrohm Model 838 Compact Ion Chromatograph). Dissolved organic carbon (DOC) was quantified on a Shimadzu TOC-5000 analyzer.

Geospatial and Remote Sensing Analysis

We characterized the spatial and physical attributes of the study lakes and their catchments using ArcMap 10 (ESRI, Redlands, California, USA). We first combined 10-m resolution digital elevation models (DEM) and the National Hydrologic Dataset within the Spatial Analyst tool framework and then delineated areas of internal drainage and water accumulation in the DEM in order to assign a flow path to each grid cell. These estimates of flow direction and accumulation were integrated across the DEM and overlaid on the National Hydrological Dataset layer to determine "pour points" for delineating catchments. We used this approach to delineate the catchments for each lake, and then we reviewed those generated polygon boundaries against 1:24,000 USGS topographic maps and aerial photography to ensure accuracy. Within each catchment, we extracted lake elevation from the DEM and determined lake morphometry (lake surface area, maximum length, and perimeter) from the National Hydrological Dataset. Although it is well established that percent wetland area within a catchment can be an important driver of lake MeHg concentrations (Shanley and others, 2005), many of these catchments had limited wetland coverage, and geospatial wetland inventories lacked the resolution necessary to conduct statistically robust analyses. Therefore, we did not address wetland influences in this study.

In order to assess landscape-level influences on fish THg concentrations, we estimated forest structure within the catchment of each lake. We used 30-m resolution grid-based forest composition and structure data derived from the Gradient Nearest Neighbor imputation methods of Ohmann and Gregory (2002). Data were acquired from the Landscape Ecology, Modeling, Mapping, and Analysis team (*http://www.fsl.orst.edu/lemma/*). The Gradient Nearest Neighbor models provide estimates for forest parameters, such as basal area, tree density, stand age, and cover class (fig. 5). Using the output from these geospatial models, we characterized the total basal area (m^2/ha) of conifers ($\geq$ 2.5 cm diameter at breast height [dbh]) within the catchment of each lake (fig. 6). Basal area is a common metric of forest structure that is related to both the density and size distribution of trees in an area. Basal area is generally correlated with canopy cover, but can be a better estimate of tree biomass because it is less sensitive to variation due to crown overlap.

Statistical Analyses

Our statistical approach was designed to both quantify the spatial variability of fish THg concentrations among lakes and regions in the WWNF, and to evaluate the relationships between fish THg concentrations and key ecological, limnological, and landscape variables across the study lakes. To do this, we employed a 2-tiered statistical approach using mixed-effects general linear models. This process allowed us to statistically control for individual-level factors that influence fish THg concentrations (such as species, fish size, and body condition) in order to generate comparable model estimates of lake-specific least-square mean fish THg concentrations. These lake-specific means could then be used to test relative importance of the landscape and limnological variables on those THg concentrations.

Our primary goal in our first tier analysis was to make comparisons of fish THg concentrations among lakes. To do this we needed to statistically control for the effects of species, fish length, and fish body condition. We excluded lake trout (N=1 from a single lake) and cutthroat trout (N=11 from a single lake) from the analysis because they only were sampled from one lake and we could not make inferences across the sampling area. We used a mixed-effects, nested general linear model with region and lake (nested within region) included as fixed factors, and relative condition factor (K_n), standard length (SL), and $\delta^{13}C$ as covariates. We also included a species x SL interaction term in the model in order to test whether the relationship between THg concentrations and fish size differed among species. Species was included as a random effect because we were limited in the number of lakes from which rainbow trout and brook were sampled together. Because our primary goal was to make comparisons of fish THg concentrations among lakes, and not necessarily to compare Hg concentrations between species, we simply needed to statistically control for the effect of species across lakes. Doing so using a fixed-effects model would have biased our lake-specific least-square mean estimates. However, we also were interested in testing for differences in THg concentrations between species where they co-occurred. Therefore, we constructed a second, fixed-effects model using a subset of the data from lakes where rainbow trout and brook trout co-occurred. Although we measured $\delta^{15}N$ ratios in the muscle fish samples, we were unable to collect baseline invertebrate samples for each lake, and thus could not make estimates of $\delta^{15}N$-derived trophic level effects on fish THg concentrations among lakes (Post, 2002). Therefore, we excluded $\delta^{15}N$ from our primary model, and instead evaluated the relationship between $\delta^{15}N$ and THg concentrations on an individual-lake basis using linear regression.

In order to examine the relationships between landscape factors and fish THg concentrations, we used the lake-specific least-square mean fish THg concentrations from the primary global model described above to statistically account for the simultaneous varying effects of fish species, fish size, and body condition, providing standardized estimates of fish Hg concentrations among lakes. We used these estimates as the response variables in general linear models, following an information-theoretic framework (Burnham and Anderson, 2002) using R software (R Development Core Team, 2011), to determine the model structure and variables that most influenced Hg bioaccumulation in these subalpine lakes. We built and ranked separate competing *a priori* candidate models to understand how fish THg concentrations varied in response to select physical and chemical variables of lakes and their catchments. Physical variables included lake surface area (km^2), lake elevation (m), lake catchment area (km^2), and the lake area:catchment area ratio. We also included the remotely sensed estimates of the basal area (m^2/ha) of conifers ≥2.5cm dbh within each lake's catchment. This commonly used silvicultural index integrates conifer stand density, age, and size to provide an approximation of conifer

7

biomass within lake catchments. Lake chemical variables included pH, acid neutralizing capacity (ANC; µeq/L), sulfate (SO_4; mg/L), and dissolved organic carbon (DOC; mg/L). We also included an intercept only model and a global model. Mercury concentrations were natural log transformed to improve residual normality. Because we lacked water chemistry data from 30 percent of our lakes, we first considered models from the reduced sample size where we had both chemical and physical data (N=18). We then conducted a similar analysis using the larger lake sample size for which we had only the physical parameter measurements (N=26).

We used Akaike's information criterion adjusted for small samples sizes (AICc) and considered the model with the lowest AICc value to be the most parsimonious (Burnham and Anderson, 2002). We included all possible variable combinations to ensure a balanced design to facilitate comparison of variable weights. However, to ensure that the number of parameters in each model did not exceed what was appropriate for our samples size, we limited the total number of variables simultaneously included in any given model to four. We determined the relative ranking of each model by subtracting each candidate model's AICc value from the best model (ΔAICc). Candidate models were considered to be competitive when ΔAICc ≤ 2.0. We calculated Akaike weights (w_i) to assess the weight of evidence that the selected model was the best candidate model (Burnham and Anderson, 2002). We also calculated variable weights by summing Akaike weights across all models that included the variable to assess the relative importance of each variable. We calculated model-averaged beta coefficient estimates from all candidate models (Burnham and Anderson, 2002).

Unless stated otherwise, all data are presented as back-transformed least-square means from model output, and standard error values are estimated using the Delta method (Williams and others, 2002).

Results

Descriptive Summary Results

We collected and analyzed a total of 327 fish, comprised of 4 species from 28 individual lakes, across 5 regions in the WWNF (table 2). Across all regions, lakes, and fish lengths, the geometric mean (± standard error) fish THg concentrations (µg/g dw) were 0.23±0.01 in brook trout (N=230), 0.17±0.01 in rainbow trout (N=85), 0.24±0.03 in cutthroat trout (N=11), and 2.13 in lake trout (N=1). We found substantial variation among lakes in the univariate relationships between THg concentrations and fish length (fig. 7), age (fig. 8), relative condition (K_n; fig. 9), $\delta^{13}C$ (fig. 10), and $\delta^{15}N$ (fig. 11). In general, we found positive correlations with $\delta^{15}N$, fish length, and age, but the relationships were inconsistent across lakes. Conversely, we generally found negative correlations with K_n. The lack of consistency in these relationships is likely due to the fact that each of these important factors were not simultaneously accounted for in the univariate analyses due to limited statistical power.

Spatial Patterns and Size Effects

Fish THg concentrations differed among regions ($F_{4, 262.7} = 60.26$, $P < 0.001$), as well as among lakes nested within region ($F_{22, 252.3} = 15.62$, $P < 0.001$). Fish THg concentrations were highest in the North Elkhorn (0.367 ± 0.032) and Seven Devils (0.320 ± 0.035) regions and lowest in the North Eagle Cap region (0.129 ± 0.011; fig. 12).

Lake-specific THg concentrations ranged from 0.040 ± 0.007 in Aneroid Lake (North Eagle Cap) to 0.718 ± 0.111 in Black Lake (North Elkhorn). Variation in fish THg concentrations generally was high in lakes both within, and among regions. Within regions, THg concentrations varied by approximately 5.6-fold in North Eagle Cap lakes, 5-fold in North Elkhorn lakes, 2.6-fold in South Elkhorn lakes, 2.4-fold in South Eagle Cap lakes, and 1.7-fold in Seven Devils lakes (fig. 13). In fact, even some lakes within less than 1 km from each other differed by up to a factor of 2.

After statistically controlling for the simultaneous effects of lake, region, standard length, and $\delta^{13}C$, fish THg concentrations were negatively correlated with the relative condition factor of individual fish ($F_{1,282.8} = 25.96$, P < 0.001; fig. 14). In fact, modeled THg concentrations decreased 3-fold across the range of fish condition factors. Across species, we did not find a relationship between THg concentrations and fish standard length ($F_{1,272.2} = 0.64$, P = 0.43). However, the significant species x SL interaction term ($F_{1,177.8} = 7.19$, P = 0.008), indicates that the rate of increase in Hg per unit length of fish differed between brook trout and rainbow trout. Finally, we found no influence $\delta^{13}C$ on fish THg concentrations across the study area ($F_{1,282.9} = 0.56$, P = 0.45), indicating that bentho-pelagic coupling was relatively unimportant to fish Hg bioaccumulation in these lakes.

When we applied a modified version of the model above (including species as a fixed effect, and adding a species x lake interaction) to a subset of lakes (Crater Lake, Fish Lake, LaGrande, Ruth Lake, and Van Pattern Lake) for which we had adequate sample sizes of brook trout and rainbow trout, we found that THg concentrations differed between species ($F_{1,88} = 10.69$, P = 0.0016), but the significant interaction between species and lake ($F_{4,88} = 34.05$, P < 0.0001) confounded our ability to appropriately interpret the main effect of species. Instead, Tukey's pairwise tests indicate that THg concentrations were higher in brook trout than rainbow trout from Fish Lake and Ruth Lake, whereas they were higher in rainbow trout than brook trout in La Grande Reservoir. We found no statistical difference between species from Van Patten or Crater Lakes (fig. 15).

Landscape and Lake Effects

The most parsimonious model explaining least-squares mean fish THg concentrations in lakes of the WWNF contained basal area of conifers within a lake's catchment, SO_4, lake area, and DOC. No other models were well supported (all ΔAICc > 2), the top model had an Akaike weight of 0.56 and was 1.6 times more likely than the next model, which was identical to the top model with the exception that it did not include DOC (table 3).

Additionally, 87 percent of the variability in our data could be explained using the top model, whereas the next best model explained only 71 percent. Using variable weights to assess the relative importance of each variable (Burnham and Anderson, 2002), models containing basal area of conifers had a combined AICc weight of 0.99, followed by SO_4 (0.96), and lake area (0.93), with moderate model support for DOC (0.57), and little evidence for effects of ANC (0.10), catchment area (0.06), pH (0.05), elevation (0.03), or the lake area to catchment ratio (0.03).

Although the variable weight for DOC was moderate, the model averaged beta coefficient estimates for this variable had 95-percent confidence intervals that slightly overlapped zero indicating that DOC (β = -0.141 ± 0.172) had a smaller effect on fish THg concentrations than did basal area (β = 0.075 ± 0.032), SO_4 (β = -0.329 ± 0.150), or lake area (β = -4.855 ± 2.803). Using model-averaged estimates, the average basal area within a lake's catchment had an overriding influence on the fish THg concentrations, resulting in a 428 percent increase in fish THg concentrations from the catchment with the lowest to the catchment with the highest conifer biomass (fig. 16). Mercury concentrations also decreased by 24, 72, and 30 percent across the observed ranges of lake area, SO_4, and DOC data, respectively (fig. 17).

Because we had a larger dataset of lakes for which only physical variables were available (N=26 vs. N=18), we also examined the influence of physical variables alone on the larger dataset. In this case, the most parsimonious model explaining fish THg concentrations again contained catchment basal area and lake surface area (table 4). No other models were well supported (all $\Delta AICc > 2$), the top model had an Akaike weight of 0.51 and was more than 4 times more likely than the next best model, which also included the ratio of lake area to catchment area (table 4). Models containing catchment basal area had a combined AICc weight of 0.97, followed by lake area (0.94), highlighting the overriding importance of those two variables in controlling fish THg concentrations in the absence of lake chemistry information. We found little evidence for effects of catchment area (0.19), elevation (0.18), or the lake area:catchment ratio (0.18). Importantly, by excluding the lake chemistry data, we reduced the predictive power of our model to explain only 47 percent of the variability in the data.

Discussion

Across the 28 subalpine lakes that we sampled in the WWNF, we found wide variation in THg concentrations of fishes, both within and among lakes. We evaluated the individual variation in fishes within lakes in the context of ecological and physiological drivers, such as foraging ecology (stable isotope-based indices) and body condition, and the among-lake differences within the context of limnological and catchment drivers, such as water chemistry and catchment forest structure. Using this hierarchical approach, we found that drivers at both scales are important in determining fish Hg bioaccumulation and risk to wildlife and humans. Additionally, these findings suggest that management options may exist at both scales that could be implemented to address mercury issues in lake ecosystems. However, further research is needed in order to better develop and test these approaches, and identify the circumstances in which they may be successful. Finally, fish THg concentrations were relatively low in WWNF lakes and comparable to other high elevation sites worldwide, but there were still common exceedances of some wildlife risk thresholds.

Mercury bioaccumulation in fishes can be influenced by a broad range of ecological and biological factors. The propensity of MeHg to bind strongly with sulfhydryl proteins in biological tissue results in long-term accumulation in protein rich tissues, such as muscle, driving a positive relationship between Hg and fish age (Evans and others, 2005). Many fish species also undergo ontogenetic diet shifts as they grow (Luczkovich and others, 1995), enabling them to target larger prey that often have higher Hg concentrations. Thus, the relationship between fish size and Hg concentrations generally is influenced by both age and trophic position (Wiener and others, 1990; Cabana and Rasmussen, 1994). However, fish Hg concentrations also are influenced by a fish's growth rate (Trudel and Rasmussen, 2006), and thus their body condition. Specifically, THg concentrations in fishes decline with faster growth because the rate of biomass accretion exceeds the assimilation and retention of dietary Hg (Stafford and others, 2004). This means that even if two fish accumulate the same total burden of Hg, the faster growing fish will have lower concentrations due simply to dilution with its own biomass (Stafford and others, 2004). Similarly, fish condition (mass relative to length) also can influence Hg concentrations by concentrating or diluting Hg burdens. Importantly, a common complication in interpreting fish

THg concentrations is the fact that fish age, body size, trophic position, and body condition are often correlated with one another to different degrees, meaning that they can influence the apparent relationships between each of these factors and fish THg concentrations. This is apparent here where we found inconsistent relationships between THg concentrations and age, length, $\delta^{15}N$, and relative condition factor across the WWNF lakes we sampled. However, after controlling for size, trophic, and site effects, we found a consistent and strong relationship between fish body condition and THg concentrations across the study region. Our results show that regardless of species, THg concentrations decreased with increasing body condition. In fact, across a 2.2-fold range of relative condition factors (0.64–1.42), we found nearly a 3-fold decrease in fish THg concentrations. This highlights the potential importance of fish body condition in determining THg concentrations, as well as the need to use care in interpreting Hg concentrations in fish populations without information on the variability in body condition. This is a notable finding because body condition in fishes varies with many factors, such as stocking density, food availability, and water quality. These factors, along with body condition itself, are commonly targeted for fisheries management, providing a potential opportunity for management applications that address both fisheries and Hg risk needs. This could be particularly valuable in environments such as subalpine lakes where Hg loading is primarily from atmospheric sources that cannot be readily managed at a local or regional scale, or in other habitats where there are logistical impediments to managing factors related to MeHg production.

Atmospheric deposition is the primary source of Hg to remote areas, such as the WWNF (Phillips and others, 2011). This is particularly true of high-elevation lakes that are largely rain and snow-fed, and lie within relatively small catchments with limited upland transport from stream networks. Mercury deposition within the region containing the WWNF has not been directly measured, but models suggest that it is elevated in comparison to much of the Pacific Northwest (U.S. Environmental Protection Agency, 2008). This is likely due to both elevated precipitation associated with orographic effects, as well as a mixture of the global background signal with more regional and localized sources. Notably, the Ash Grove cement plant in Durkee, Oregon lies within the region surrounding the WWNF, and is approximately 60 km from the closest study lake. Prior to the recent implementation of Hg controls in their processes, the plant was among the largest emitters of Hg in the western United States (Schmeltz and others, 2011). However, the magnitude of current or historical Hg deposition from the plant to the subalpine catchments of the WWNF is unclear because no direct deposition measurements are available. Moreover, atmospheric deposition models such as REMSAD (U.S. Environmental Protection Agency, 2008), provide only a 12 km resolution, which is too coarse to incorporate lake-specific deposition estimates into our modeling results. Importantly, spatial variability in fish THg concentrations was substantial among WWNF lakes. Least-square mean fish THg concentrations in lakes (statistically controlling for species and size effects) varied by nearly 3-fold within regions, and by 18-fold across the entire study area. However, it is uncertain whether Hg loadings to the lakes exhibit similar variability, which would indicate very dynamic atmospheric vectors of Hg deposition. An important next step is to determine if sediment Hg concentrations mimic the trends in fish THg concentrations. Certainly source magnitude is an important driver of Hg bioaccumulation in aquatic food webs, but as these data suggest, only within the context of the ecological and biogeochemical factors driving MeHg production and the speciation of inorganic Hg.

The physical and chemical characteristics of lakes and their catchments have long been linked with fish Hg concentrations because of their role in facilitating MeHg production, or in controlling Hg entry and transport through the food web (Snodgrass and others, 2000). Factors that are commonly important include wetland area, lake size, lake productivity, forest coverage, DOC, pH, and sulfate (Greenfield and others, 2001; St. Louis and others, 2004; Hall and others, 2005; Driscoll and others, 2007; Shanley and others, 2012). However, aside from percentage of wetland area and pH, conflicting data exist on the degree and direction of impact for many of the other parameters. Consistent with other studies, fish THg concentrations from lakes in the WWNF were strongly predicted by a combination of landscape and limnological factors. In fact, 87 percent of the variability in lake-specific least-squares mean fish THg concentrations could be explained using a model containing (1) lake water DOC concentrations, (2) lake water sulfate concentrations, (3) lake surface area, and (4) average basal area of conifers within the lake's catchment. Interestingly, we found negative relationships between fish THg concentrations and both sulfate and DOC. Because sulfate is a key component in the MeHg production process, dissolved SO_4 concentrations are often positively correlated with MeHg concentrations in water, sediments, and biota (Mitchell and others, 2008). However, at high sulfate concentrations in reducing conditions, the rapid reduction to sulfide can subsequently inhibit MeHg production, resulting in a negative correlation (Benoit and others, 1999; Mehrotra and Sedlak, 2005; Windham-Myers and others, 2009). Interestingly, the sulfate concentrations in WWNF lakes ranged from 0.17 to 7.9 mg/L, with a median concentration of only 0.36 mg/L, making this an unlikely explanation. Thus, more intensive limnological and geochemical research across the study lakes would be necessary to more fully explain this relationship.

The role of DOC in the Hg cycle is complex (Lambertsson and Nilsson, 2006). Dissolved organic matter not only facilitates Hg transport through watersheds (Shanley and others, 2008), but also can enhance or reduce biological uptake (Wiener and others, 2006; Dutton and Fisher, 2012), as well as serve as a carbon source for microbial activity, increasing MeHg production rates (Lambertsson and Nilsson, 2006). The complexity of the role played by DOC in these processes is driven by both its quantity and composition (Shanley and others, 2012). We found negative correlations between DOC and fish THg concentrations across our study lakes, which is consistent with studies in midwestern seepage lakes where DOC in the water column commonly inhibits biological uptake of MeHg (Wren and others, 1991). This result by itself is not surprising given the fact that the lakes we studied in WWNF lacked inflowing streams and were primarily fed through precipitation, catchment snowmelt, and groundwater. However, the strong positive influence of catchment vegetation (conifer basal area) on fish THg concentrations suggests the potential for a greater catchment influence, one where carbon supplied to the lake by the catchment may drive Hg bioaccumulation. Specifically, conifer basal area within a lake's catchment was overwhelmingly the most important factor that we measured in driving the variation in fish THg concentrations among lakes. In fact, model-averaged fish THg concentrations ranged from 0.11 to 0.58 µg/g dw between the lakes with the lowest and highest basal areas. This is a novel finding with the potential for wide-ranging implications in the management of Hg in forested catchments.

Previous studies have identified forests as important components to the Hg cycling at the landscape scale, where Hg varies positively with percentage of area of large watersheds that are forested (Driscoll and others, 2007). Trees accumulate Hg from the atmosphere within their leaf tissue and also provide surface area for Hg deposition and adsorption to leaf surfaces (Graydon and others, 2009; Tebatchnick and others, 2012). Additionally, the organic and litter horizons in forest soils are major sites of Hg storage, particularly in association with soil organic matter (Obrist and others, 2011). To our knowledge no other study has quantified a key forest structure metric such as basal area at such a fine spatial resolution within a catchment in relation to biological Hg concentrations. The mechanism behind this relationship is not yet clear, but may be due to either enhanced carbon delivery associated with more organic-rich soils, elevated Hg scavenging from the atmosphere in tree needles, or a combination of both. It is beyond the scope of this work to determine these mechanisms, but clearly identifies a key need for future research in forested watersheds.

Organisms, such as fish from high-elevation lakes, serve as important indicators for understanding how background concentrations and atmospheric deposition may be influencing remote environments. Additionally, they provide a unique opportunity to test for the influence of natural landscape characteristics on Hg cycling within lakes. The THg concentrations of fishes from lakes in the WWNF generally are lower than those of other remote, high-elevation lakes worldwide (fig. 18). Interestingly, in comparison with other high-elevation lakes from National Parks in the western United States, average concentrations in WWNF fishes ranged from 1.4 times higher than fish Glacier National Park, to 2.2 times lower than fish from Mount Rainier National Park. The causes for these differences are unclear, but given our results on the importance of lake chemistry and catchment characteristics, they could be due some combination of these factors as well as differences in Hg deposition flux.

Further research is needed in order to better understand the relative importance of those other drivers, particularly interdisciplinary studies that incorporate measurements of Hg deposition, flux and speciation in the abiotic components of each catchment in combination with bioaccumulation dynamics. The THg concentrations in WWNF fishes were all below the EPA's human health criteria of 0.3 µg/g ww in the fillet, except for the lone lake trout sampled from Lookinglass Lake. However, when assessed relative to a suite of wildlife health thresholds, 2, 10, 25, and 68 percent of fishes sampled exceeded the whole body (ww) thresholds for common loon reproductive impairment (0.18 µg/g ww; Depew and others, 2012), common loon behavioral alterations (0.1 µg/g ww; Depew and others, 2012), and protection of mink (0.7 µg/g ww; Lazorchak and others, 2003), and kingfisher (0.03 µg/g ww; Lazorchak and others, 2003), respectively. Whether there are taxa within the forest that are being impacted, and the potential degree of impact is uncertain and would require further study.

Acknowledgments

This study was funded by the U.S. Department of Agriculture Forest Service, the U.S. Geological Survey Forest and Rangeland Ecosystem Science Center, and the U.S. Geological Survey Environmental Health Mission Area. This study would not have been possible without many dedicated field hours from a number of people. In particular, we appreciate the support of David Salo, Alan Miller, Bob Rock, Leigh Woodruff, Mary Ellen Emerick, Holly Akenson, Amy Busch, Randi Jandt, Tim Bailey, and Jeff Yanke. We also are grateful for the efforts of Kevin Donner, John Pierce, Brandon Kowalski, and Nick Baker for their laboratory efforts; Jack Landers and Kiira Siitari for otolith preparation and reading; and Patti Haggerty for her expertise and guidance on geospatial analyses. We also thank David Salo, Alan Miller, Martin Fitzpatrick, and Leigh Woodruff for comments on previous versions of the report.

References Cited

Anderson, R.O., and Neumann, R.M., 1996, Length, weight, and associated structural indices, *in* Murphy, B.R. and Willis, D.W., eds., Fisheries Techniques, 2nd ed.: Bethesda, Maryland, American Fisheries Society, p. 447–482.

Benoit, J.M., Gilmour, C.C., Mason, R.P., Heyes, A., 1999, Sulfide controls on mercury speciation and bioavailability in sediment pore waters: Environmental Science and Technology, v. 33, p. 951-957.

Blais, J.M., Charpentie, S., Pick, F., Kimpe, L.E., Amand, A.S., Regnault-Roger, C., 2006, Mercury, polybrominated duphenyl ether, organochlorine pesticide, and polychlorinated biphenyl concentrations in fish from lakes along an elevation transect in the French Pyrenees: Ecotoxicology and Environmental Safety, v.63, p. 91-99.

Bloom, N.S., 1992, On the chemical form of mercury in edible fish and marine invertebrate tissue: Canadian Journal of Fisheries and Aquatic Science, v. 49, p. 1010–1017.

Burnham, K.P., and Anderson, D.R., 2002, Model Selection and Multimodel Inference: A Practical Information-Theoretic Approach, 2nd ed.: New York, Springer-Verlag.

Cabana, G., and Rasmussen, J.B., 1994, Modeling food chain structure and contaminant bioaccumulation using stable nitrogen isotopes: Nature, v. 372, p. 255-257.

Depew, D.C., Basu, N., Burgess, N.M., Campbell, L.M., Evers, D,C,, Grasman, K.A., and Scheuhammer, A.M., 2012, Derivation of screening benchmarks for dietary methylmercury exposure for the common loon (*Gavia Immer*): Rationale for use in Ecological Risk Assessment: Environmental Toxicology and Chemistry, v. 31, p. 2399-2407.

Driscoll, C.T., Han Y., Chen, C., Evers, D., Lambert, K., Holsen, T., Kamman, N., and Munson, R., 2007, Mercury contamination in remote forest and aquatic ecosystems in the northeastern U.S.: Sources, transformations and management options: Bioscience, v. 57, p.17-28.

Dutton, J., and Fisher, N.S., 2012, Influence of humic acids on the uptake of aqueous metals by the killifish *Fundulus heteroclitus*: Environmental Toxicology and Chemistry, v. 31, p. 2225-2232.

Eagles-Smith, C.A., Suchanek, T.H., Colwell, A.E., and Anderson, N.L., 2008, Mercury trophic transfer in a eutrophic lake: the importance of habitat-specific foraging: Ecological Applications, v. 18, p. A196- A212.

Engstrom, D.R., Balogh, S.J., and Swain, E.B., 2007, History of mercury inputs to Minnesota lakes: Influence of watershed disturbance and localized atmospheric deposition: Limnology and Oceanography, v. 52, p. 2467-2483.

Evans, M.S., Lockhart, W.L., Doetzel, L., Low, G., Muir, D., Kidd, K., Stephens, G., and Delaronde, J., 2005, Elevated mercury concentrations in fish in lakes in the Mackenzie River Basin: the role of physical, chemical, and biological factors: Science of the Total Environment, v. 351–352, p. 479–500.

Friedli, H.R., Radke, L.F., Prescott, R., Hobbs, P.V., and Sinha, P., 2003, Mercury emissions from the August 2001 wildfires in Washington State and an agricultural waste fire in Oregon and atmospheric mercury budget estimates: Global Biogeochemical Cycles, v. 17, p. 1039.

Gran, G., 1952, Determination of the equivalence point in potentiometric titrations--Part II: The Analyst, v. 77, p. 661-671.

Graydon, J.A., St. Louis, V.L., Hintelmann, H.H., Lindberg, S.E., Sandilands, K.A., Rudd, J.W.M., Kelly, C.A., Tate, M.T., Krabbenhoft, D.P., and Lehnherr, I., 2009, Investigation of uptake and retention of atmospheric Hg(II) by boreal forest plants using stable Hg isotopes: Environmental Science and Technology, v. 43, p. 4960-4966.

Greenfield, B.K., Hrabik, T.R., Harvey, C.J., and Carpenter, S.R., 2001, Predicting mercury
    levels in yellow perch: use of water chemistry, trophic ecology, and spatial traits: Canadian
    Journal of Fisheries and Aquatic Sciences , v. 58, p. 1419-1429.
Hall, B.D., St. Louis, V.L., Rolfhus, K.R., Bodaly, R.A., Beaty, K.G., Paterson, M.L., and
    Cherewyk, K.A., 2005, Impacts of reservoir creation on the biogeochemical cycling of methyl
    mercury and total mercury in boreal upland forests: Ecosystems, v. 8, p. 248–266.
Hobson, K.A., and Bairlein, F., 2003, Isotopic fractionation and turnover in captive Garden
    Warblers (*Sylvia borin*): implications for delineating dietary and migratory associations in wild
    passerines: Canadian Journal of Zoology, v. 81, p. 1630–1635.
Jenssen, M.T.S., Borgstrom, R., Salbu, B., Rosseland, B.O., 2010, The importance of size and
    growth rate in determining mercury concentrations in European minnow (*Phoxinus phoxinus*)
    and brown trout (*Salmo trutto*) in the subalpine lake, Ovre Heimdalsvatn: Hydrobiologia,
    v. 642, p. 115-126.
Lambertsson, L., and Nilsson, M., 2006, Organic material: The primary control on mercury
    methylation and ambient methyl mercury concentrations in estuarine sediments:
    Environmental Science and Technology, v. 40, p. 1822-1829.
Landers, D.H., Simonich, S.L., Jaffe, D.A., Geiser, L.H., Campbell, D.H., Schwindt, A.R.,
    Schreck, C.B., Kent, M.L., Hafner, W.D., Taylor, H.E., Hageman, K.J., Usenko, S., Ackerman,
    L.K., Schrlau, J.E., Rose, N.L., Blett, T.F., Erway, M.M., 2008, The Fate, Transport, and
    Ecological Impacts of Airborne Contaminants in Western National Parks (USA). EPA/600/R-
    08/138. U.S. Environmental Protection Agency, Office of Research and Development,
    NHEERL, Western Ecology Division, Corvallis, Oregon.
Lazorchak, J.M., McCormick, F.H., Henry, T.R., and Herlihy, A.T., 2003, Contamination of fish
    in streams of the mid-Atlantic region: an approach to regional indicator selection and wildlife
    assessment: Environmental Toxicology and Chemistry, v. 22, p. 545-553.
Lindberg, S., Bullock, R., Ebinghaus, R., Engstrom, D., Feng, X.B., and Fitzgerald, W., 2007, A
    synthesis of progress and uncertainties in attributing the sources of mercury in deposition:
    Ambio, v. 36, p. 19–32.
Luczkovich, J.J., Norton, S.F., and Gilmore G.R., 1995, The influence of oral anatomy on prey
    selection during the ontogeny of two percoid fishes, *Lagadon rhomboids* and *Centropornus
    undecimalis:* Environmental Biology of Fishes, v. 44, p. 79-95.
Maruszczak, N., Larose, C., Dommergue, A., Paquet, S., Beaulne, J., Maury-Brachet, R., Lucotte,
    M., Nedjai, R., Ferrari, C., 2011, Mercury and methylmercury concentrations in high altitude
    lakes and fish (Arctic charr) from the French Alps related to watershed characteristics: Science
    of the Total Environment, v. 409, p. 1909-1915.
Mason, R.P., Fitzgerald, W.F., and Morel, F.M., 1994, The biogeochemical cycling of elemental
    mercury: Anthropogenic influences: Geochimica et Cosmochimica Acta, v. 58, p. 3191-3198.
Mehrotra A.S., and Sedlak, D.L., 2005, Decrease in net mercury methylation rates following iron
    amendment to anoxic wetland sediment slurries: Environmental Science and Technology, v.
    39, p. 2564-2570.
Mitchell, M.J., Bailey, S.W., Shanley, J.B., and Mayer, B., 2008, Evaluating sulfur dynamics
    during storm events for three watersheds in the northeastern USA: A combined hydrological,
    chemical and isotopic approach: Hydrological Processes, v. 22, p. 4023-4034.
Moran, P.W., Aluru, N., Black, R.W., Vijayan, M.M., 2001, Tissue contaminants and associated
    transcriptional response in trout liver from high elevation lakes of Washington: Environmental
    Science and Technology, v. 41, p. 6591-6597.

Obrist, D., Johnson, D.W., Lindberg, S.E., Luo, Y., Hararuk, O., Bracho, R., Battles, J.J., Dail, D.B., Edmonds, R.L. Monson, R.K., Ollinger, S.V., Pallardy, S.G., Pregitzer, K.S., and Todd, D.E., 2011, Mercury distribution across 14 U.S. Forests. Part I: Spatial patterns of concentrations in biomass, litter, and soils: Environmental Science and Technology, v. 45, p. 3974-3981.

Ohmann, J.L., and Gregory, M.J., 2002, Predictive mapping of forest composition and structure with direct gradient analysis and nearest-neighbor imputation in coastal Oregon, U.S.A.: Canadian Journal of Forest Research, v. 32, p. 725–741.

Phillips, J.A., Louis, V.L., Cooke, C.A., Vinebrooke, R.D., and Hobbs, W.O., 2011, Increased mercury loadings to western Canadian Alpine lakes over the past 150 years: Environmental Science and Technology, v. 45, p. 2042-2047.

Pirrone, N., Cinnirella, S., Feng, X., Finkelman, R.B., Friedli, H.R., Leaner, J., Mason, R., Mukherjee, A.B., Stracher, G.B., Streets, D.G., and Telmer, K., 2010, Global mercury emissions to the atmosphere from anthropogenic and natural sources: Atmospheric Chemistry and Physics Discussions, v. 10, p. 4719–4752.

Post, D.M., 2002, Using stable isotopes to estimate trophic position: models, methods, and assumptions: Ecology, v. 83, p. 703-718.

R Development Core Team, 2011, R: A language and environment for statistical computing. R Foundation for Statistical Computing, Vienna, Austria. ISBN 3-900051-07-0, accessed April 15, 2013, at http://www.R-project.org/.

Rasband, W.S., 1997, ImageJ: U.S. National Institutes of Health, Bethesda, Maryland, USA, accessed April 15, 2014, at http://imagej.nih.gov/ij/.

Rudd, J.W.M., 1995, Sources of methylmercury to freshwater ecosystems: A review: Water Air Soil Pollution, v. 80, p. 697-713.

Scheuhammer, A.M., Meyer, M.W., Sandheinrich, M.B., and Murray, M.W., 2007, Effects of environmental methylmercury on the health of wild birds, mammals, and fish: Ambio, v. 36, p. 12-18.

Schmeltz, D., Evers, D., Driscoll, C., Artz, R., Cohen, M., Gay, D., Haeuber, R., Krabbenhoft, D.P., Mason, R., Morris, K., and Wiener, J.G., 2011, MercNet: a national monitoring network to assess responses to changing mercury emissions in the United States: Ecotoxicology, v. 20, p. 1713-1725.

Secor, D.H., Dean, J.M., and Laban, E.H., 1991, Manual for otolith removal and preparation for microstructural examination: Belle W. Baruch Institute, University of South Carolina Press, Columbia, SC, p. 85.

Shanley, J.B., and Chalmers, A.T., 2012, Streamwater fluxes of total mercury and methylmercury into and out of Lake Champlain: Environmental Pollution, v. 161, p. 311-320.

Shanley, J.B., Mast, M.A., Campbell, D.H., Aiken, G.R., Krabbenhoft, D.P., Hunt, R.J., Walker, J.F., Schuster, P.F., Chalmers, A., Aulenbach, B.T., Peters, N.E. Marvin-DiPasquale, M.,., Chow, D.W., and Shafer, M.M., 2008, Comparison of total mercury and methylmercury cycling at five sites using the small watershed approach: Environmental Pollution, v. 154, p. 143-154.

Shanley, J.B., Kamman, N.C., Clair, T.A., Chalmers, A., 2005, Physical controls on total and methylmercury concentrations in streams and lakes of Northeastern USA: Ecotoxicology, v. 14, p. 125-134.

Snodgrass, J.W., Jagoe, C.H., Bryan, A.L., Brant, H.A., and Burger, J., 2000, Effects of trophic status and wetland morphology, hydroperiod, and water chemistry on mercury concentrations in fish: Canadian Journal of Fisheries and Aquatic Sciences, v. 57, p. 171-180.

Stafford, C.P., Hanson, B., and Stanford, J.A., 2004, Mercury in fishes and their diet items from Flathead Lake, Montana: Transactions of the American Fisheries Society, v. 133, p. 349-357.

St. Louis, V.L., Rudd, J.W.M., Kelly, C.A., Beaty, K.G., Bloom, N.S., and Flett, R.J., 1994, Importance of wetlands as sources of methyl mercury to boreal forest ecosystems: Canadian Journal of Fisheries and Aquatic Science, v. 51, p. 1065-1076.

St. Louis, V.L., Rudd, J.W.M., Kelly, C.A., Bodaly, R.A., Patterson, M.J., Beaty, K., Hesslein, R., Hayes, A., and Majewski, A., 2004, The rise and fall of mercury methylation in an experimental reservoir: Environmental Science and Technology, v. 38, p. 1348-1358.

Tebatchnick, M.D., Nogaro, G., and Hammerschmidt, C.R., 2012, Potential sources of methylmercury in tree foliage: Environmental Pollution, v. 160, p. 82-87.

Trudel, M., and Rasmussen, J. B., 2006, Bioenergetics and mercury dynamics in fish: a modeling perspective: Canadian Journal of Fisheries and Aquatic Sciences, v. 63, p. 1890-1902.

U.S. Environmental Protection Agency, 2000, Method 7473, Mercury in solids and solutions by thermal decomposition, amalgamation, and atomic absorption spectrophotometry, Test methods for evaluating solid waste, physical/chemical methods SW846, Update IVA. Printing Office (GPO), Washington, DC, USA.

U.S. Environmental Protection Agency, 2008, Model-based analysis and tracking of airborne mercury emissions to assist in watershed planning: accessed April 15, 2013, at *http://www.epa.gov/owow/tmdl/pdf/final300report_10072008.pdf.*

Wiener, J.G., Knights, B.C., Sandheinrich, M.B., Jeremiason, J.D., Brigham, M.E., Engstrom, D.R., Woodruff, L.G., Cannon, W.F., and Balogh, S.J., 2006, Mercury in soils, lakes, and fish in Voyageurs National Park (Minnesota): Importance of atmospheric deposition and ecosystem factors: Environmental Science and Technology, v. 40, p. 6261-6268.

Wiener, J.G., Martini, R.E., Sheffy, T.B., and Glass, G.E., 1990, Factors influencing mercury concentrations in walleyes in northern Wisconsin lakes: Transactions of the American Fisheries Society, v. 119, p. 862-870.

Williams, B.K., Nichols, J.D., and Conroy, M.J., 2002, Analysis and management of animal populations—Modeling, estimation, and decision making: San Diego, California, Academic Press, p. 817.

Windham-Myers, L., Marvin-Dipasquale, M., Krabbenhoft, D.P., Agee, J.L., Cox, M.H., Heredia-Middleton, P., Coates, C., and Kakouros, E., 2009, Experimental removal of wetland emergent vegetation leads to decreased methylmercury production in surface sediment: Journal of Geophysical Research, v. 114.

Wren, C.D., Scheider, W.A., Wales, D.L., Muncaster, B.W., and Gray, I.M., 1991, Relation between mercury concentration in walleye (*Stizostedion vitreum vitreum*) and northern pike (*Esox Lucius*), in Ontario lakes and influence of environmental factors: Canadian Journal of Fisheries and Aquatic Sciences, v. 48, p. 132-139.

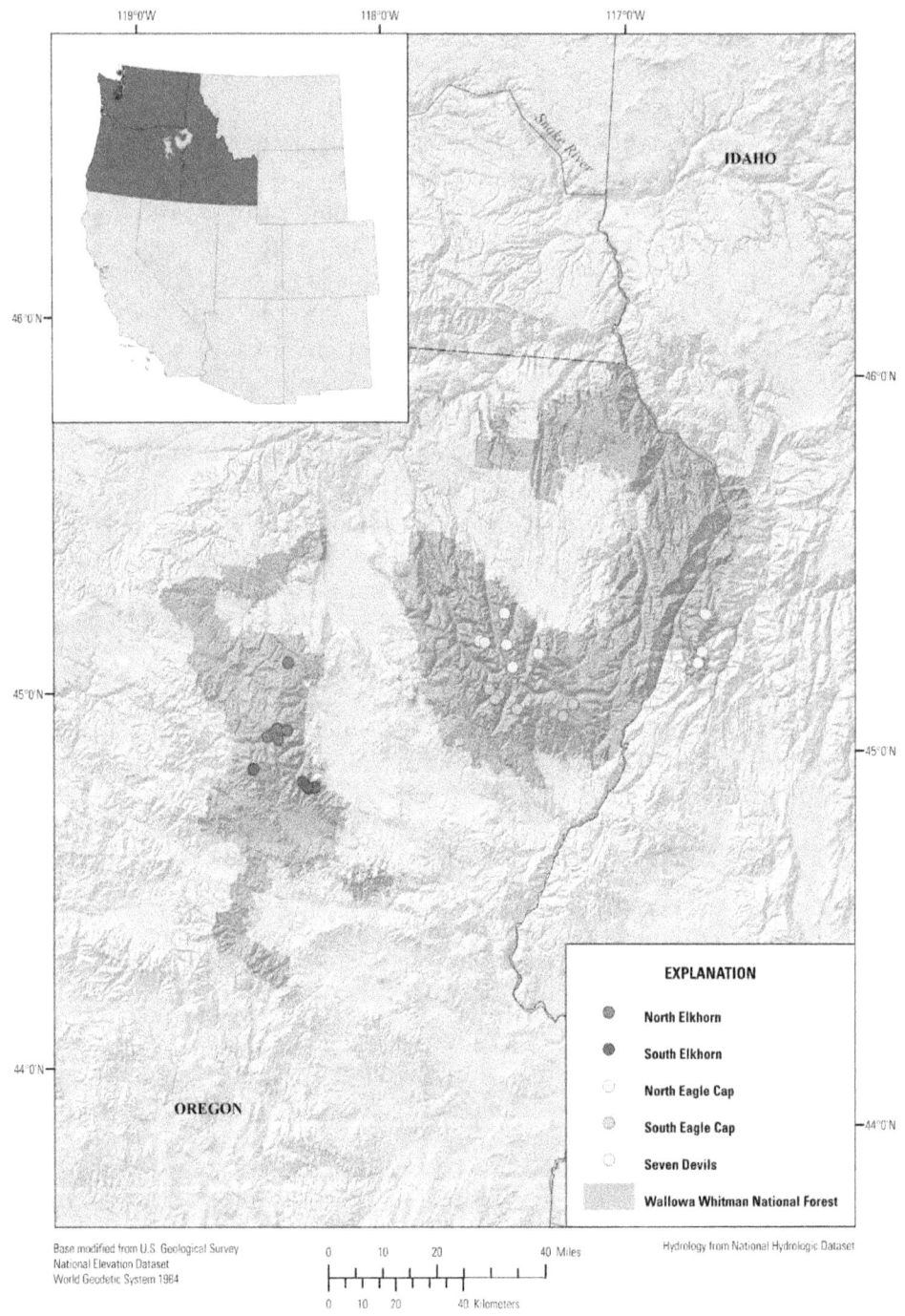

Figure 1. Map of the Wallowa-Whitman National Forest in northeastern Oregon and western Idaho. Colored symbols represent lakes sampled in various regions of the National Forest.

Figure 2. Goodrich Lake and its catchment in the South Elkhorn Range. Inset: Sampled brook trout.

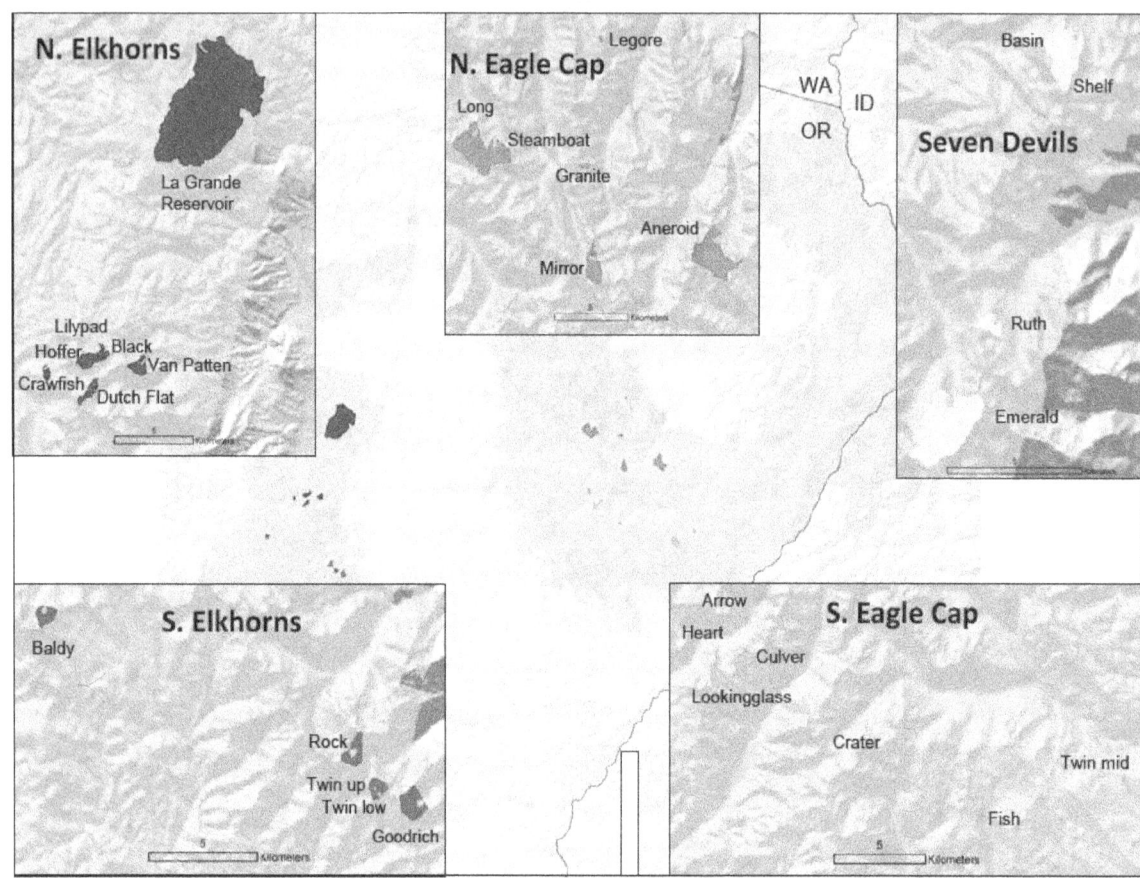

Figure 3. Locations of study lakes and their respective catchments (defined by colored polygons) within each region (N. Elkhorns [red], S. Elkhorns [blue], N. Eagle Cap [green], S. Eagles Cap [orange], and Seven Devils [yellow]) in the Wallowa-Whitman National Forest, northeastern Oregon and western Idaho.

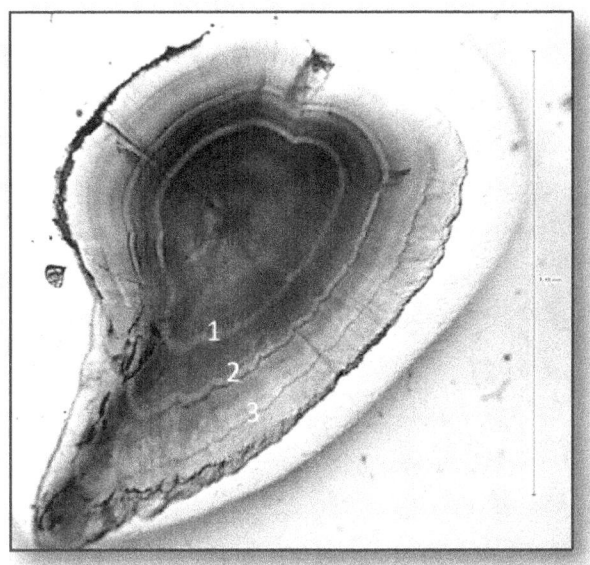

Figure 4. Digital image of a brook trout sagittal otolith, showing annular rings.

Figure 5.   Visual examples of gradients in catchment forest structure in the Wallowa-Whitman National Forest, northeastern Oregon and western Idaho.

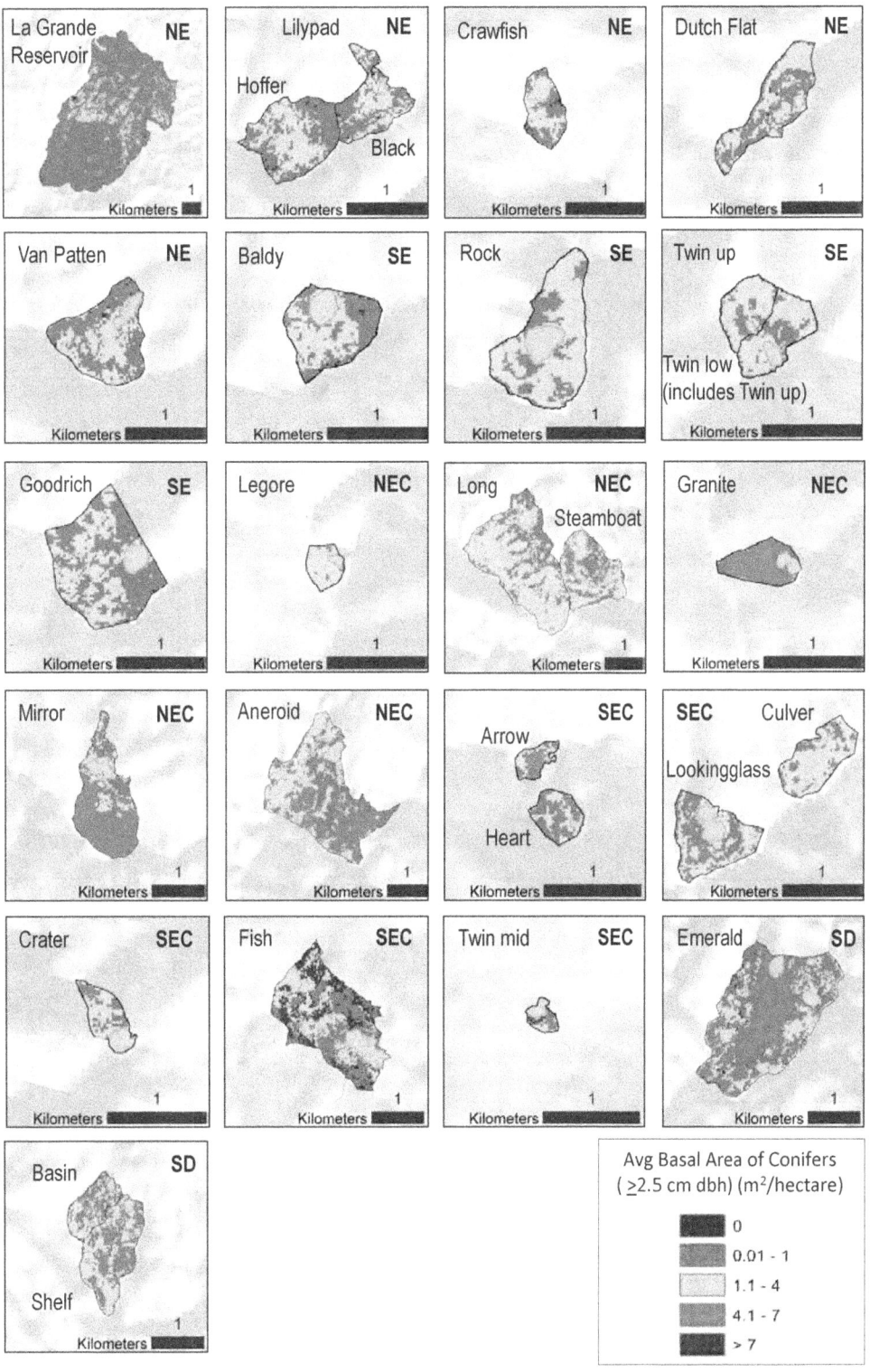

Figure 6. Conifer density measured as basal area (m²/hectare) of all conifers >2.5 cm dbh for Wallowa-Whitman National Forest lake catchments, northeastern Oregon and western Idaho. Regions in bold: NE=North Elkhorn, SE=South Elkhorn, NEC=North Eagle Cap, SEC=South Eagle Cap, SD=Seven Devils. Note, incomplete data for Ruth Lake catchment.

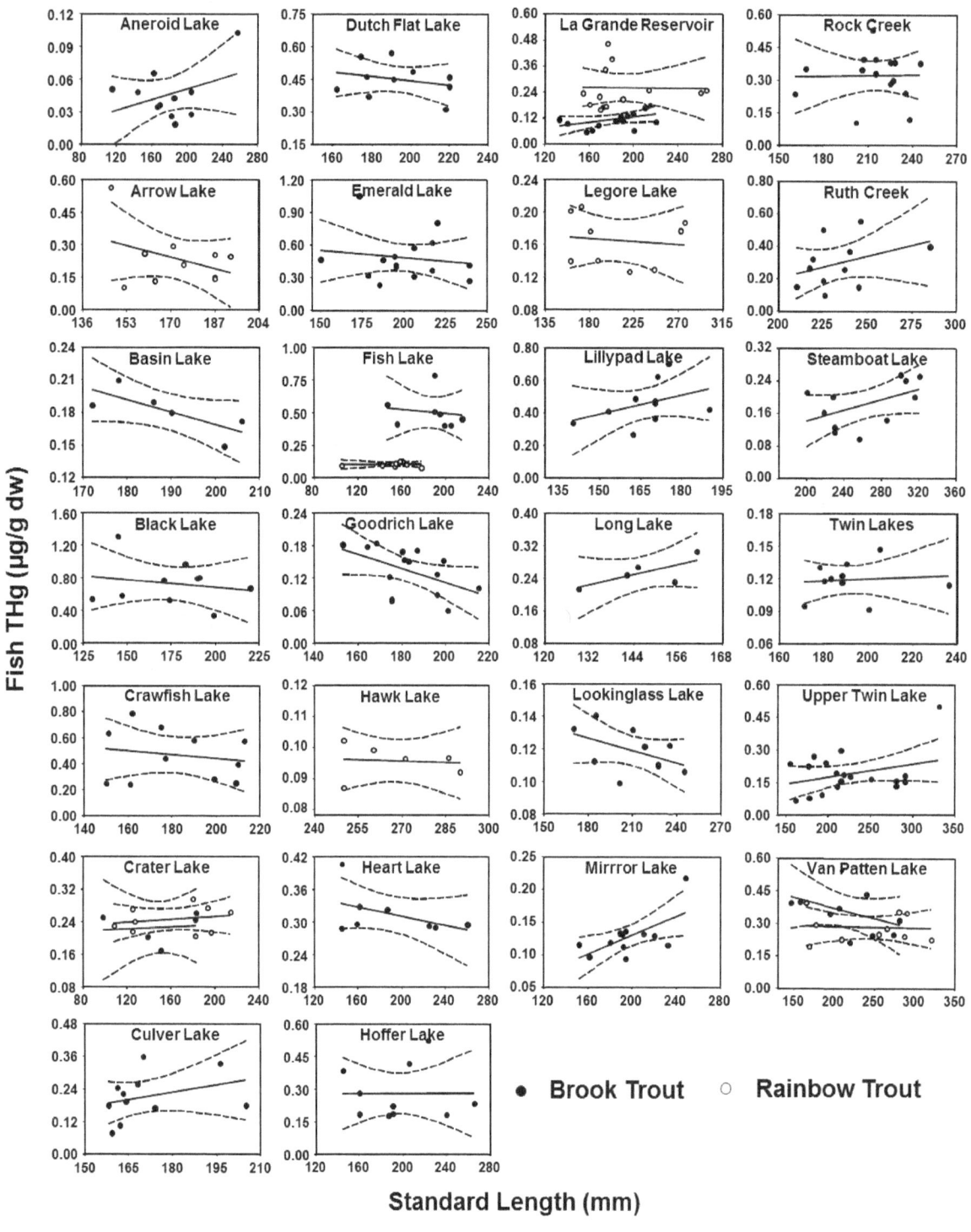

Figure 7. Linear relationships between total mercury (THg) concentrations (dw = dry weight concentration) in fish muscle, and fish size (standard length) from different lakes in the Wallowa-Whitman National Forest, northeastern Oregon and western Idaho. Closed circles represent brook trout (*Salvelinus fontinalis*), and open circles represent rainbow trout (*Oncorhynchus mykiss*).

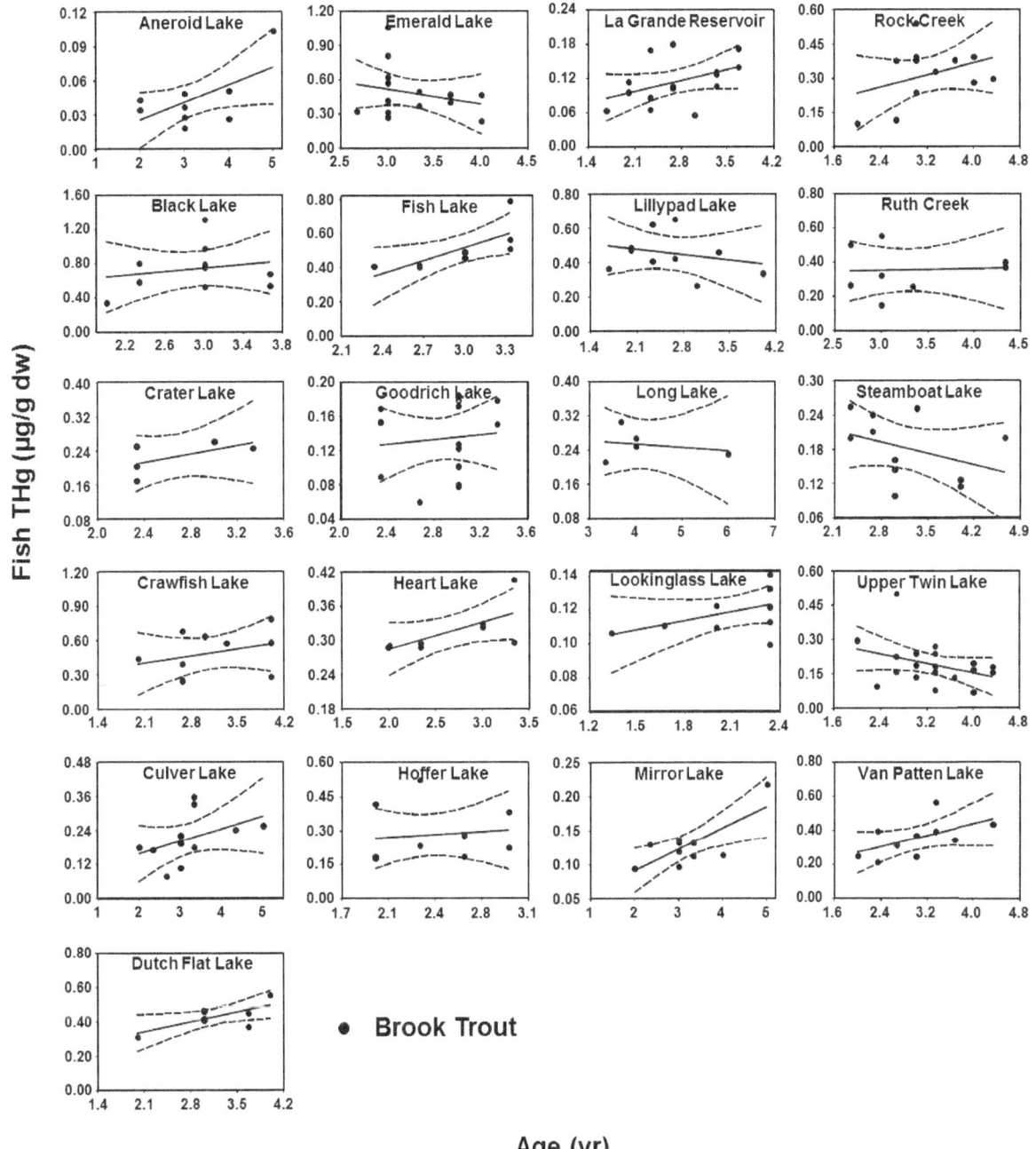

Fish THg (µg/g dw)

Age (yr)

Figure 8. Linear relationships between total mercury (THg) concentrations (dw = dry weight) in fish muscle, and fish age (estimated by counting sagittal otolith annuli) from select lakes in the Wallowa-Whitman National Forest, northeastern Oregon and western Idaho. Results are provided for 21 lakes because some lakes did not contain brook trout.

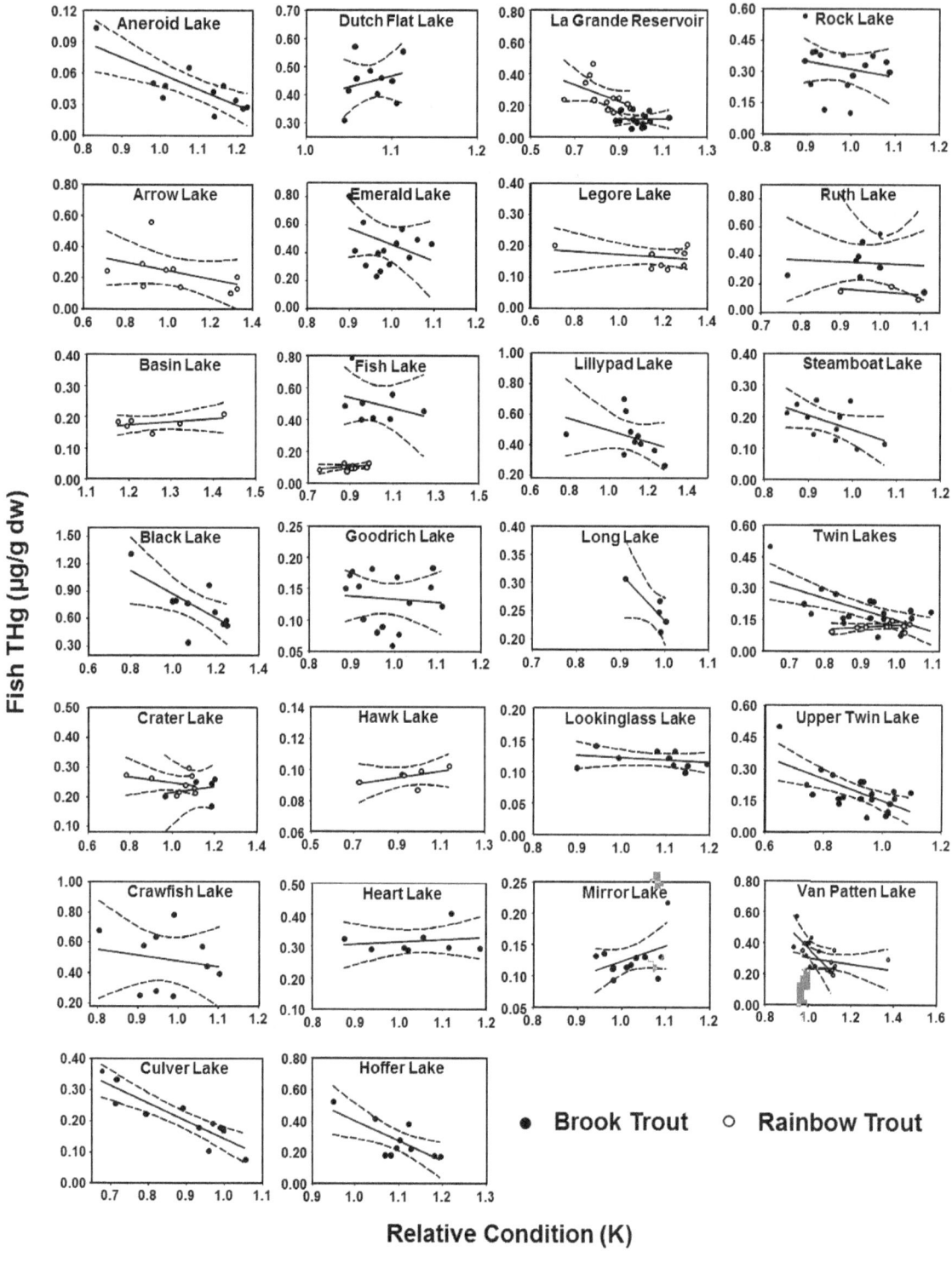

Figure 9. Linear relationships between total mercury (THg) concentrations (dw = dry weight) in fish muscle, and relative condition factor from different lakes in the Wallowa-Whitman National Forest, northeastern Oregon and western Idaho. Closed circles represent brook trout (*Salvelinus fontinalis*), and open circles represent rainbow trout (*Oncorhynchus mykiss*).

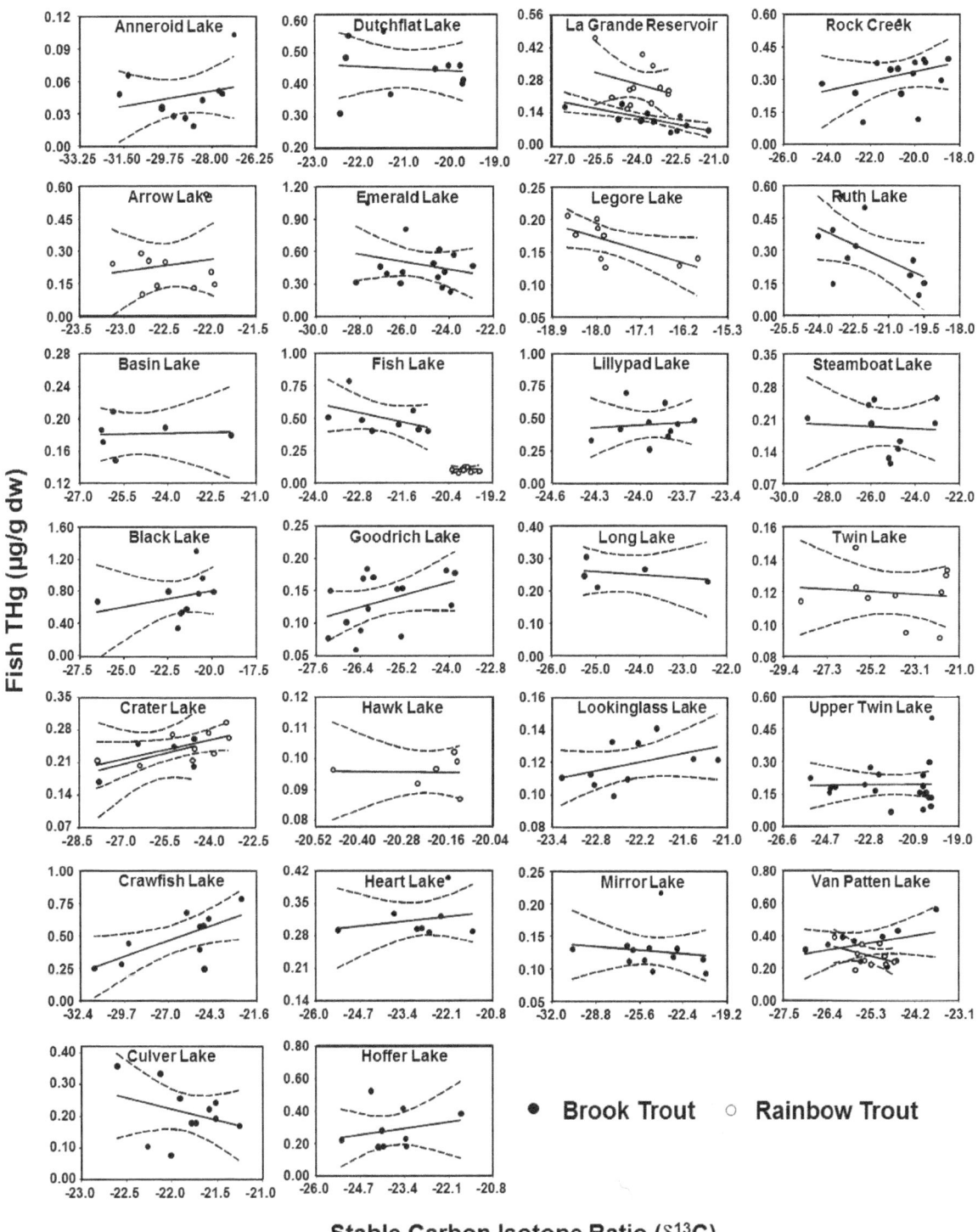

Figure 10. Linear relationships between total mercury (THg) concentrations (dw = dry weight) in fish muscle, and stable carbon isotope ratios from different lakes in the Wallowa-Whitman National Forest, northeastern Oregon and western Idaho. Closed circles represent brook trout (*Salvelinus fontinalis*), and open circles represent rainbow trout (*Oncorhynchus mykiss*).

27

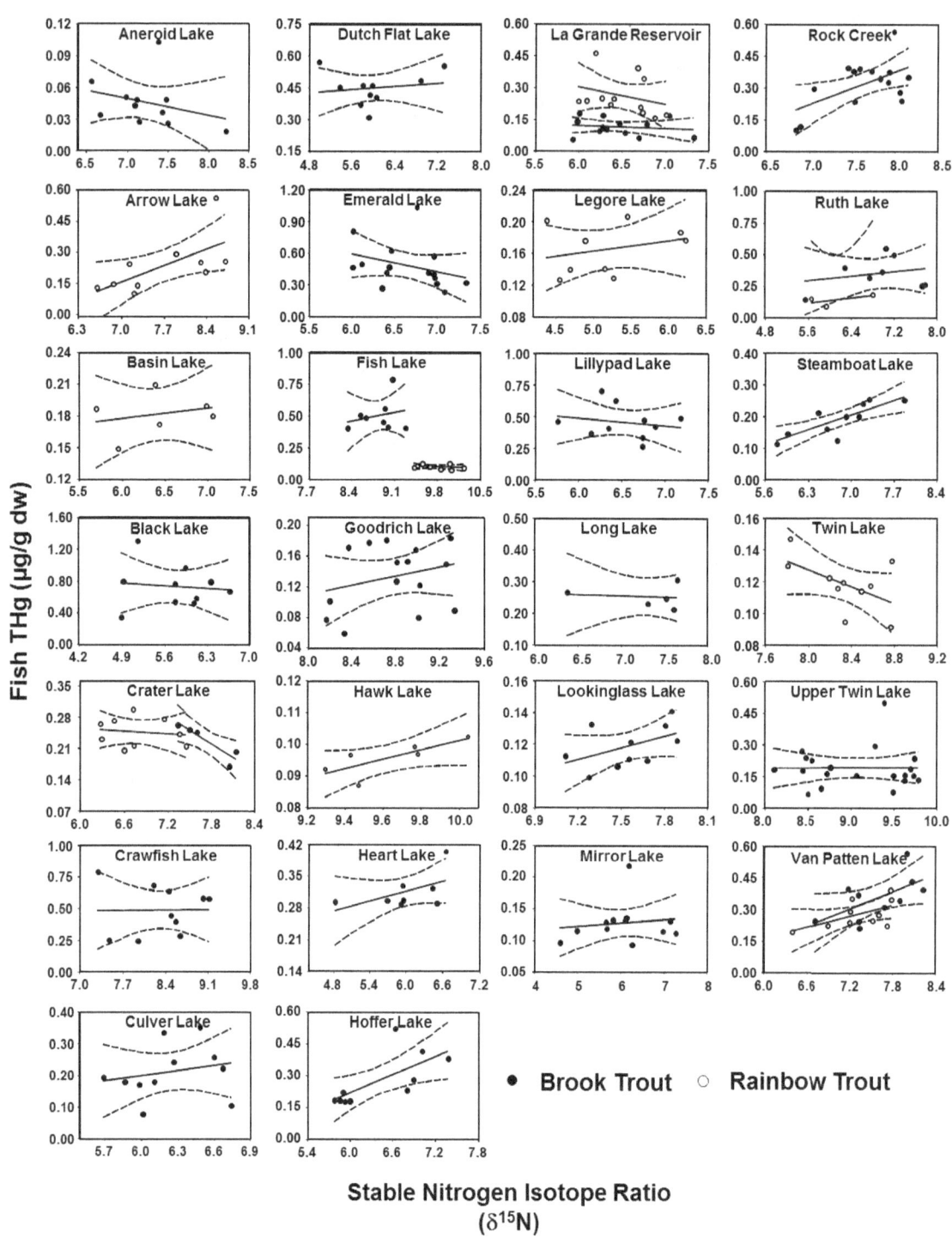

Figure 11. Linear relationships between total mercury (THg) concentrations (dw = dry weight) in fish muscle, and stable nitrogen isotope ratios from different lakes in the Wallowa-Whitman National Forest, northeastern Oregon and western Idaho. Closed circles represent brook trout (*Salvelinus fontinalis*), and open circles represent rainbow trout (*Oncorhynchus mykiss*).

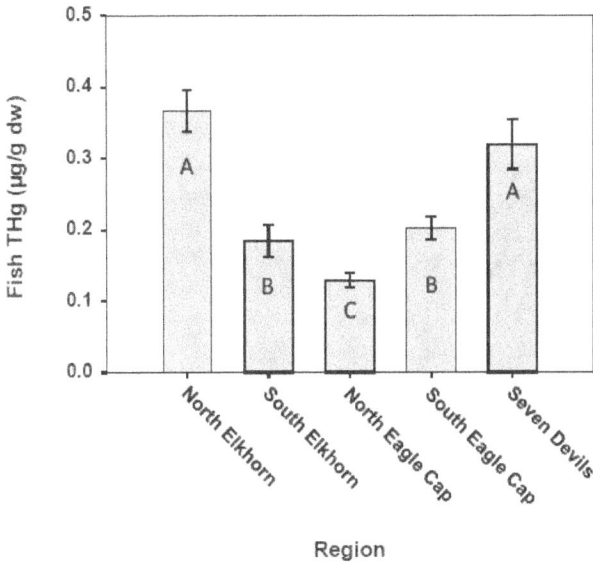

Figure 12. Back transformed least-square mean fish muscle total mercury (THg) concentrations for the 5 study regions in the Wallowa-Whitman National Forest. Differing letters among bars indicate statistically significance differences in THg concentrations at alpha = 0.05

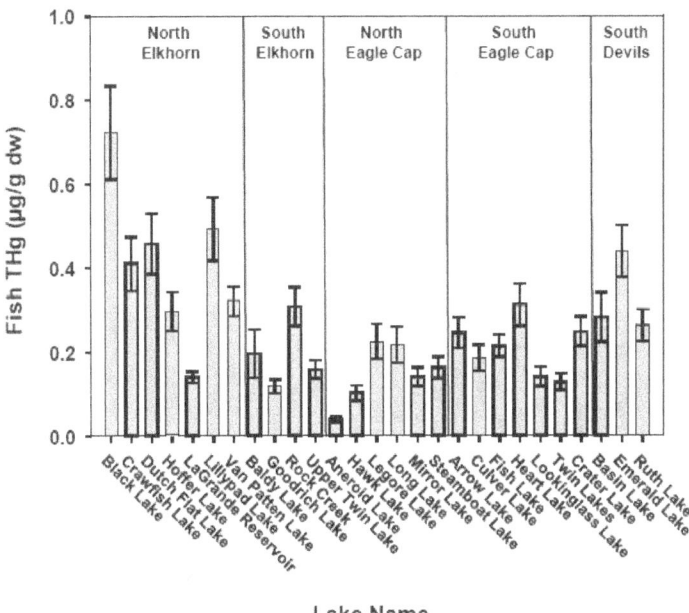

Figure 13. Back transformed least-square mean fish muscle total mercury (THg) concentrations for the 27 study lakes in the Wallowa-Whitman National Forest, northeastern Oregon and western Idaho.

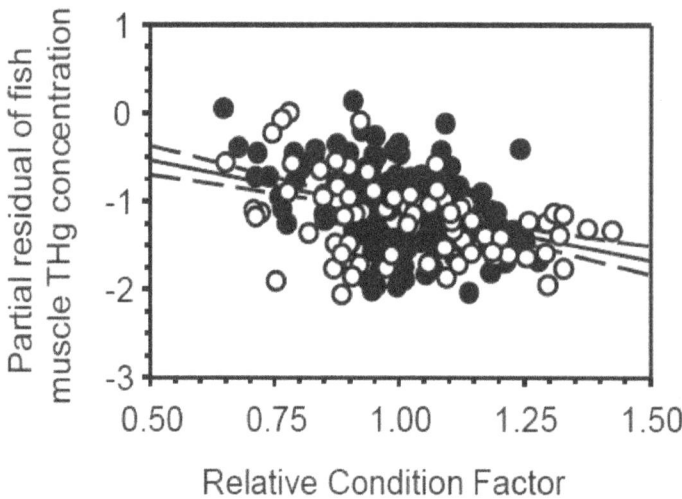

Figure 14. Partial residual plot of fish total mercury (THg) concentrations in relation to relative condition factor. Solid circles indicate brook trout, open circles represent rainbow trout. Partial residuals are derived from the global mixed-effects general linear model that includes lake, region, fish length, and $\delta^{13}C$.

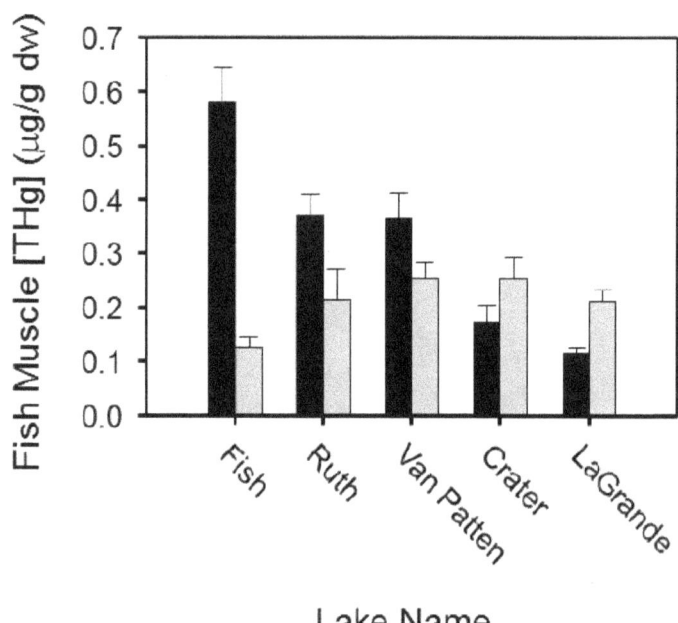

Figure 15. Fish muscle total mercury (THg) concentrations in brook trout (*Salvelinus fontinalis*; black bars) and rainbow trout (*Oncorhynchus mykiss*; gray bars) from five lakes where they co-occurred in the Wallowa-Whitman National Forest, northeastern Oregon and western Idaho.

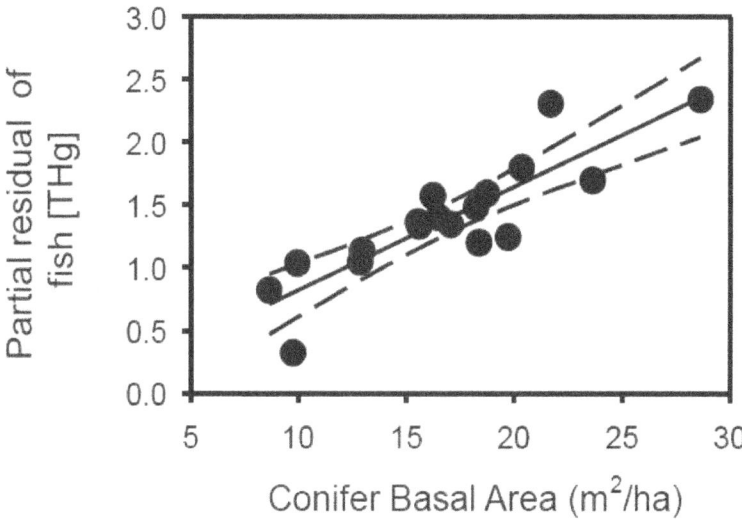

Figure 16. Relationship between conifer (>2.5 cm diameter at breast height) basal area within a lake's catchment on fish THg concentrations. Data are plotted as partial residuals from the best model to adjust for the effects of other independent factors on fishTHg concentrations. Each data point represents a single lake.

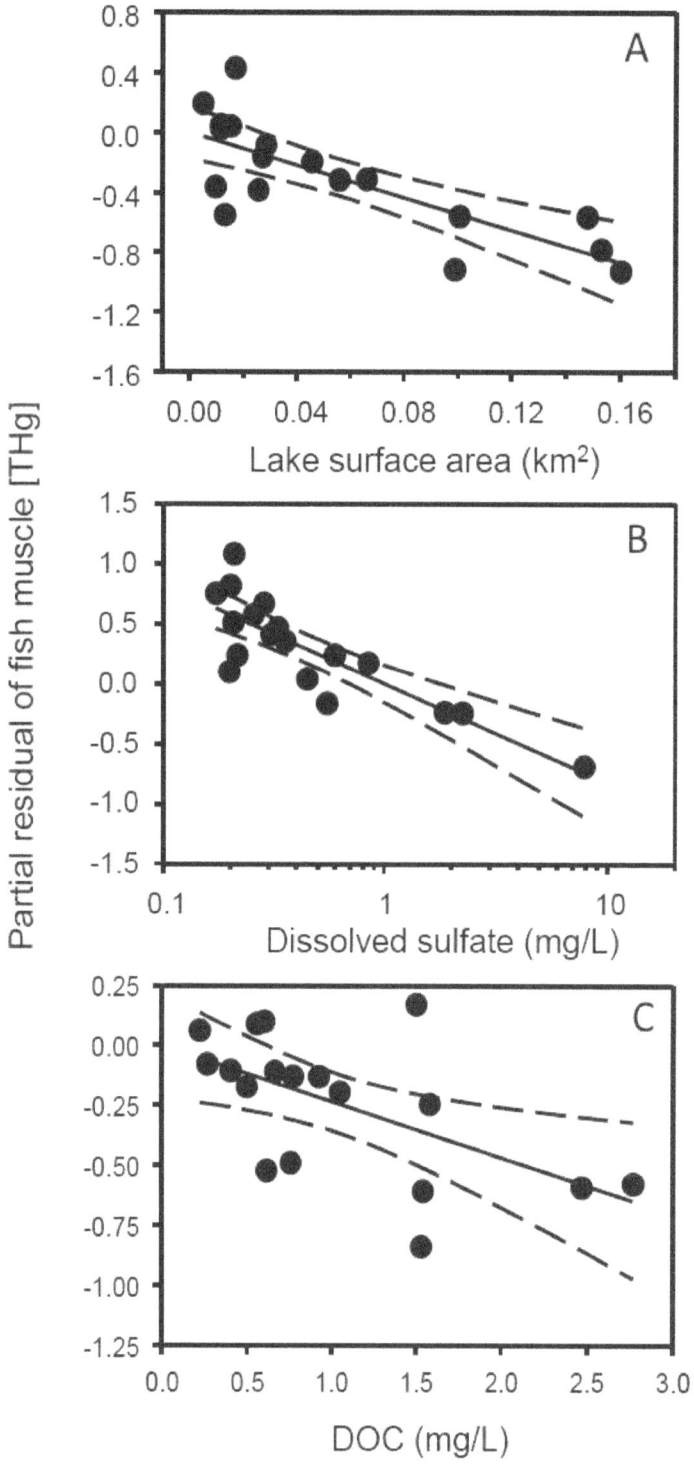

Figure 17. Influence of (A) lake surface area, (B) dissolved sulfate, and (C) dissolved organic carbon on fish THg concentrations in the Wallowa-Whitman National Forest, northeastern Oregon and western Idaho. Data are plotted as partial residuals from the best model to adjust for the effect of other independent factors on fish THg concentrations.

32

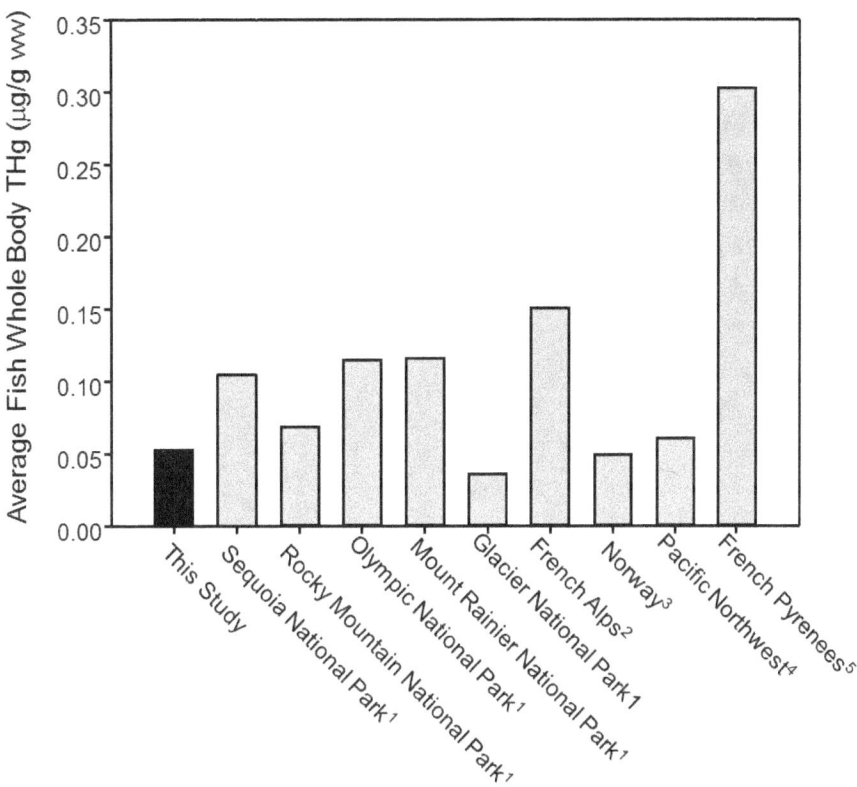

Figure 18. Mean total mercury (THg) concentrations in salmonid fishes from other high-elevations lakes in comparison to this study. [1]Landers and others, 2008; [2]Marusczak and others, 2011; [3]Jenssen and others, 2010; [4]Moran and others, 2007; [5]Blais and others, 2006.

Table 1. Chemical and physical attributes of study lakes and their catchments in the Wallowa-Whitman National Forest, northeastern Oregon and western Idaho.

[[a]% of catchment area; [b]bm²/ha, diameter at breast height >2.5cm; BRTR = Brook trout, RATR = Rainbow trout, LATR = Lake trout, CUTR = Cutthroat trout]

Region	Lake Name	Latitude	Longitude	Elevation (m)	Lake Surface Area (km²)	Catchment Area (km²)	Canopy Cover[a]	Basal Area[b]	Fish Species
N. Eagle Cap	Aneroid Lake	45.208873	-117.203488	2286	0.1531	5.425	44.73	15.59	BRTR, RATR
N. Eagle Cap	Granite/Hawk Lake	45.231943	-117.330740	2436	0.0131	0.263	31.88	9.75	RATR
N. Eagle Cap	Legore Lake	45.310301	-117.346113	2725	0.0116	0.130	27.12	8.63	RATR
N. Eagle Cap	Long Lake	45.233449	-117.439989	2169	0.1479	4.763	45.39	16.22	BRTR
N. Eagle Cap	Mirror Lake	45.178258	-117.309000	2315	0.1007	1.876	38.42	12.85	BRTR
N. Eagle Cap	Steamboat Lake	45.229967	-117.417914	2244	0.1602	2.132	47.86	17.05	BRTR
N. Elkhorns	Black Lake	44.954079	-118.220636	2240	0.0169	0.499	55.08	21.68	BRTR
N. Elkhorns	Crawfish Lake	44.935206	-118.265268	2101	0.0559	0.368	59.19	28.61	BRTR
N. Elkhorns	Dutch Flat Lake	44.930837	-118.220282	2238	0.0152	0.769	45.91	20.35	BRTR
N. Elkhorns	Hoffer Lake	44.949454	-118.236193	2278	0.0096	0.864	53.03	18.36	BRTR
N. Elkhorns	LaGrande Reservoir	45.137065	-118.201446	1558	0.1189	31.891	52.86	25.01	BRTR, RATR
N. Elkhorns	Lilypad Lake	44.957612	-118.226323	2179	0.0084	0.071	60.97	28.96	BRTR
N. Elkhorns	Van Patten Lake	44.955503	-118.185464	2254	0.0593	0.971	51.67	20.58	BRTR, RATR
S. Eagle Cap	Arrow Lake	45.109944	-117.393089	2386	0.0051	0.099	30.72	9.94	RATR
S. Eagle Cap	Crater Lake	45.058066	-117.275198	2301	0.0458	0.209	45.37	18.73	BRTR, RATR
S. Eagle Cap	Culver Lake	45.093022	-117.348249	2146	0.0272	0.527	51.98	18.21	BRTR
S. Eagle Cap	Fish Lake	45.046502	-117.092215	2031	0.2564	2.991	62.16	30.70	BRTR, RATR
S. Eagle Cap	Heart Lake	45.105766	-117.387880	2228	0.0116	0.195	45.11	15.52	BRTR
S. Eagle Cap	Lookinglass Lake	45.080028	-117.363020	2226	0.0989	0.747	52.91	19.71	BRTR, LATR
S. Eagle Cap	Twin Lakes	45.080853	-117.054626	1962	0.0237	0.071	44.08	22.31	RATR
S. Elkhorns	Baldy Lake	44.845230	-118.313904	2171	0.0672	0.601	58.71	28.74	BRTR
S. Elkhorns	Goodrich Lake	44.809660	-118.060431	2094	0.0661	1.266	41.65	16.47	BRTR
S. Elkhorns	Rock Creek	44.822190	-118.109395	2338	0.0968	0.924	40.7	14.79	BRTR
S. Elkhorns	Twin Lakes_Lower	44.808119	-118.086737	2335	0.0286	0.631	33.95	12.94	BRTR
Seven Devils	Basin Lake	45.344960	-116.555504	2250	0.0257	0.670	57.62	23.62	RATR
Seven Devils	Emerald Lake	45.212100	-116.570336	2072	0.0808	4.456	52.1	22.12	BRTR
Seven Devils	Ruth Lake	45.242100	-116.556800	2215	0.0326	0.476	NA	NA	BRTR, RATR
Seven Devils	Shelf Lake	45.342280	-116.550757	2275	0.0327	1.511	52.67	21.47	CUTR

34

Table 1. Chemical and physical attributes of study lakes and their catchments in the Wallowa-Whitman National Forest, northeastern Oregon and western Idaho - Continued.

[[a]ANC = acid neutralizing capacity, meq/L ; [b]Cond = conductivity, mS/cm ; [c]Anions and cations, mg/L; DOC = dissolved organic carbon, mg/L; bdl = below detection limit, NA = not analyzed]

Region	Lake Name	pH	ANC[a]	Cond[b]	Na[c]	NH4[c]	K[c]	Mg[c]	Ca[c]	F[c]	Cl[c]	SO4[c]	DOC[c]
N. Eagle Cap	Aneroid Lake	7.819	842.4	92.6	0.776	0.016	0.816	1.146	14.074	0.020	0.073	7.906	1.05
N. Eagle Cap	Granite/Hawk Lake	6.371	51	6.8	0.333	0.017	0.248	0.174	0.935	bdl	0.284	0.199	1.53
N. Eagle Cap	Legore Lake	7.16	191.1	20.4	0.598	bdl	0.326	0.285	3.225	0.015	0.070	0.848	0.222
N. Eagle Cap	Long Lake	7.094	110.9	11.2	0.426	bdl	0.275	0.193	1.822	bdl	0.051	0.201	0.601
N. Eagle Cap	Mirror Lake	7.083	100.2	10.6	0.459	bdl	0.336	0.12	1.414	bdl	0.052	0.359	0.403
N. Eagle Cap	Steamboat Lake	6.843	93	9.9	0.493	bdl	0.288	0.202	1.24	bdl	0.062	0.207	0.497
N. Elkhorns	Black Lake	6.751	132.5	13.4	0.629	bdl	0.255	0.682	1.587	bdl	0.069	0.209	1.5
N. Elkhorns	Crawfish Lake	7.104	205.6	20.3	1.061	bdl	0.42	0.359	2.87	0.015	0.175	0.307	2.47
N. Elkhorns	Dutch Flat Lake	7.264	220.4	21.2	0.966	bdl	0.284	0.412	2.801	0.013	0.052	0.173	1.58
N. Elkhorns	Hoffer Lake	6.598	95.5	9.5	0.491	bdl	0.198	0.277	1.288	bdl	0.058	0.216	0.76
N. Elkhorns	LaGrande Reservoir	NA	NA	NA	NA	NA	NA	NA	NA	NA	NA	NA	NA
N. Elkhorns	Lilypad Lake	NA	NA	NA	NA	NA	NA	NA	NA	NA	NA	NA	NA
N. Elkhorns	Van Patten Lake	NA	NA	NA	NA	NA	NA	NA	NA	NA	NA	NA	NA
S. Eagle Cap	Arrow Lake	7.081	157.9	14.5	0.607	bdl	0.525	0.23	1.982	bdl	0.067	0.285	0.557
S. Eagle Cap	Crater Lake	6.757	88.5	9.8	0.489	0.014	0.221	0.084	0.579	bdl	0.095	0.598	0.775
S. Eagle Cap	Culver Lake	6.712	110.8	16.1	0.65	bdl	0.52	0.45	1.374	bdl	0.062	1.875	0.266
S. Eagle Cap	Fish Lake	7.437	185.6	20.0	1.072	bdl	0.202	0.263	2.657	0.012	0.123	0.524	NA
S. Eagle Cap	Heart Lake	6.988	163.4	14.5	0.618	bdl	0.436	0.163	2.184	bdl	0.050	0.256	0.927
S. Eagle Cap	Lookinglass Lake	6.548	64.5	7.1	0.37	bdl	0.283	0.085	1.129	bdl	0.057	0.552	0.616
S. Eagle Cap	Twin Lakes	NA	NA	NA	NA	NA	NA	NA	NA	NA	NA	NA	NA
S. Elkhorns	Baldy Lake	NA	NA	NA	NA	NA	NA	NA	NA	NA	NA	NA	NA
S. Elkhorns	Goodrich Lake	7.686	490.3	53.6	0.695	bdl	0.352	0.797	7.454	0.022	0.077	2.248	0.664
S. Elkhorns	Rock Creek	NA	NA	NA	NA	NA	NA	NA	NA	NA	NA	NA	NA
S. Elkhorns	Twin Lakes_Lower	7.61	644.4	58.2	1.149	bdl	0.214	1.031	8.209	0.020	0.072	0.331	2.77
Seven Devils	Basin Lake	7.546	429.8	45.9	0.684	0.031	0.175	0.306	6.976	bdl	0.131	0.450	1.54
Seven Devils	Emerald Lake	7.397	244.3	29.2	1.007	bdl	0.156	0.484	1.812	0.014	0.082	2.248	NA
Seven Devils	Ruth Lake	7.074	221.6	31.4	0.608	0.011	0.158	0.286	3.531	bdl	0.113	0.416	NA
Seven Devils	Shelf Lake	NA	NA	NA	0.586	0.068	0.386	0.366	2.436	bdl	0.318	0.343	NA

35

Table 2. Fish catch data and size ranges from subalpine lakes in the Wallowa-Whitman National Forest, northeastern Oregon and western Idaho.

Lake Name	Brook trout			Rainbow trout			Cutthroat trout			Lake trout		
	SL Range (mm)	Mean SL (mm)	N	SL Range (mm)	Mean SL (mm)	N	SL Range (mm)	Mean SL (mm)	N	SL Range (mm)	Mean SL (mm)	N
Aneroid Lake	145 - 265	212.5	10	NA	290	1	--	--	--	--	--	--
Arrow Lake	--	--	--	165 - 320	238.4	10	--	--	--	--	--	--
Baldy Lake	204 - 257	230.5	2	--	--	--	--	--	--	--	--	--
Basin Lake	--	--	--	218 - 320	286.3	6	--	--	--	--	--	--
Black Lake	161 - 248	210.9	10	--	--	--	--	--	--	--	--	--
Crater Lake	245 - 276	263.6	5	250 - 290	268.2	9	--	--	--	--	--	--
Crawfish Lake	152 - 220	188.3	10	--	--	--	--	--	--	--	--	--
Culver Lake	129 - 175	154.9	11	--	--	--	--	--	--	--	--	--
Dutch Flat Lake	170 - 245	210.2	10	--	--	--	--	--	--	--	--	--
Emerald Lake	150 - 196	167.9	15	--	--	--	--	--	--	--	--	--
Fish Lake	182 - 215	201.1	8	200 - 300	244.4	9	--	--	--	--	--	--
Goodrich Lake	147 - 206	184.4	15	--	--	--	--	--	--	--	--	--
Granite/Hawk Lake	--	--	--	215 - 238	225.5	6	--	--	--	--	--	--
Heart Lake	162 - 220	198.8	8	--	--	--	--	--	--	--	--	--
Hoffer Lake	133 - 190	167.9	10	--	--	--	--	--	--	--	--	--
LaGrande Reservoir	150 - 239	199.7	15	154 - 250	202.4	12	--	--	--	--	--	--
Legore Lake	--	--	--	146 - 247	204.7	9	--	--	--	--	--	--
Lilypad Lake	160 - 220	177.1	10	--	--	--	--	--	--	--	--	--
Long Lake	205 - 220	215.8	5	--	--	--	--	--	--	--	--	--
Lookingglass Lake	105 - 178	150.1	10	--	--	--	--	--	--	659	--	1
Mirror Lake	98 - 174	138.1	12	--	--	--	--	--	--	--	--	--
Rock Creek	115 - 204	168.1	15	--	--	--	--	--	--	--	--	--
Ruth Lake	174 - 218	196.6	8	290 - 330	303.3	3	--	--	--	--	--	--
Shelf Lake	--	--	--	--	--	--	133 - 265	191.2	11	--	--	--
Steamboat Lake	125 - 209	183.9	11	--	--	--	--	--	--	--	--	--
Twin Lakes_Eagle Cap	--	--	--	210 - 285	233.2	10	--	--	--	--	--	--
Upper Twin Lakes_Elkhorns	153 - 231	175.2	20	--	--	--	--	--	--	--	--	--
Van Patten Lake	145 - 215	177.8	10	161 - 200	183.1	10	--	--	--	--	--	--

Table 3. Ranking of candidate models describing physical and chemical variables influencing fish THg concentrations in the Wallowa-Whitman National Forest, northeastern Oregon and western Idaho.

[Models presented include only those that were within 8 AICC units of the top model (ΔAICC = 0) and the null (intercept) models; [a]Variables considered included basal area, lake area, lake elevation, lake catchment area, ratio of lake area to lake catchment area, lake pH, acid neutralizing capacity (ANC), lake sulfate (SO_4), and dissolved organic carbon (DOC); [b]Number of estimated parameters in the model including the intercept and variance; [c]Second-order Akaike's Information Criterium (AICc); [d]The difference in the value between the AICc of the current model and the value of the most parsimonious model; [e] Likelihood of the model given the data, relative to candidate models; [f]The weight of the evidence that the top model is better than the selected model, given the candidate model set].

Model Structure	n	K[b]	-2LogL	AICc[c]	ΔAICc[d]	w[e]	Evidence ratio[f]	r²
Basal area + lake area + SO_4 + DOC	18	6	-1.673	17.963	0.000	0.56	1.00	0.87
Basal area + lake area + SO_4	18	5	4.986	19.986	2.023	0.20	1.58	0.71
Basal area + lake area + SO_4 + ANC	18	6	3.096	22.733	4.770	0.05	2.10	0.75
Basal area + lake area + SO_4 + catchment area	18	6	4.716	24.353	6.390	0.02	2.60	0.76
Basal area + lake area + SO_4 + elevation	18	6	4.887	24.524	6.561	0.02	2.61	0.72
Basal area + lake area + SO_4 + lake area to catchment ratio	18	6	4.960	24.596	6.634	0.02	2.89	0.72
Basal area + lake area + SO_4 + pH	18	6	4.979	24.615	6.653	0.02	2.95	0.71
Basal area + lake area + ANC + pH	18	6	5.039	24.676	6.713	0.02	2.98	0.81
Basal area + SO_4 + catchment area	18	5	10.012	25.013	7.050	0.02	3.07	0.53
Basal area + SO_4	18	4	14.518	25.596	7.633	0.01	3.40	0.50
Intercept	18	2	34.997	39.798	21.835	0.00	55130.92	-

Table 4. Ranking of candidate models describing physical variables influencing fish THg concentrations in the Wallowa-Whitman National Forest[a], northeastern Oregon and western Idaho.

Model Structure	n	K[b]	-2LogL	AICc[c]	ΔAICc[d]	w[e]	Evidence ratio[f]	r²
Basal area + lake area	26	4	30.375	40.279	0.000	0.51	1.00	0.46
Basal area + lake area + lake area to catchment ratio	26	5	30.226	43.226	2.947	0.12	4.36	0.46
Basal area + lake area + catchment area	26	5	30.309	43.309	3.029	0.11	4.55	0.46
Basal area + lake area + elevation	26	5	30.365	43.365	3.085	0.11	4.68	0.46
Basal area + lake area + catchment area + lake area to catchment ratio	26	6	30.016	46.437	6.158	0.02	21.73	0.47
Basal area + lake area + catchment area + elevation	26	6	30.047	46.468	6.189	0.02	22.07	0.47
Basal area	26	3	39.503	46.594	6.315	0.02	23.51	0.23
Basal area + lake area + lake area to catchment ratio + elevation	26	6	30.218	46.639	6.360	0.02	24.05	0.46
Intercept	26	2	46.336	50.858	10.579	0.00	198.20	-

[Model presented include only those that were within 8 AICC units of the top model (ΔAICC = 0) and the null (intercept) models; [a]Variables considered included basal area, lake area, lake elevation, lake catchment area, and ratio of lake area to lake catchment area; [b]Number of estimated parameters in the model including the intercept and variance; [c]Second-order Akaike's Information Criterium (AICc); [d]The difference in the value between the AICc of the current model and the value of the most parsimonious model; [e]Likelihood of the model given the data, relative to candidate models; [f]The weight of the evidence that the top model is better than the selected model, given the candidate model set].